Lecture Notes in Artificial Intelligence   7124

Subseries of Lecture Notes in Computer Science

LNAI Series Editors

Randy Goebel
University of Alberta, Edmonton, Canada
Yuzuru Tanaka
Hokkaido University, Sapporo, Japan
Wolfgang Wahlster
DFKI and Saarland University, Saarbrücken, Germany

LNAI Founding Series Editor

Joerg Siekmann
DFKI and Saarland University, Saarbrücken, Germany

Daniel Villatoro Jordi Sabater-Mir
Jaime Simão Sichman (Eds.)

Multi-Agent-Based Simulation XII

International Workshop, MABS 2011
Taipei, Taiwan, May 2-6, 2011
Revised Selected Papers

 Springer

Series Editors

Randy Goebel, University of Alberta, Edmonton, Canada
Jörg Siekmann, University of Saarland, Saarbrücken, Germany
Wolfgang Wahlster, DFKI and University of Saarland, Saarbrücken, Germany

Volume Editors

Daniel Villatoro
Jordi Sabater-Mir
IIIA – Artificial Intelligence Research Institute
CSIC – Spanish Scientific Research Council
Campus Universitat Autonoma de Barcelona
08193 Bellaterra, Spain
E-mail: {dvillatoro, jsabater}@iiia.csic.es

Jaime Simão Sichman
LTI – Laboratório de Técnicas Inteligentes
Universidade de São Paulo
Av. Prof. Luciano Gualberto 158 tv.3
05508-970 São Paulo SP, Brazil
E-mail: jaime.sichman@poli.usp.br

ISSN 0302-9743   e-ISSN 1611-3349
ISBN 978-3-642-28399-4   ISBN 978-3-642-28400-7 (eBook)
DOI 10.1007/978-3-642-28400-7
Springer Heidelberg Dordrecht London New York

Library of Congress Control Number: 2012931157

CR Subject Classification (1998): I.2, I.2.11, D.2, F.1, I.6, C.2.4

LNCS Sublibrary: SL 7 – Artificial Intelligence

Typesetting: Camera-ready by author, data conversion by Scientific Publishing Services, Chennai, India

Printed on acid-free paper

Springer is part of Springer Science+Business Media (www.springer.com)

Preface

The 2011 edition of the Multi-Agent-Based Simulation (MABS) workshop was the 12th occurence of a series that began in 1998. Its scientific focus lies in the confluence of social sciences and multi-agent systems, with a strong application/empirical vein, and its emphasis is placed on (a) exploratory agent-based simulation as a principled way of undertaking scientific research in the social sciences and (b) using social theories as an inspiration to new frameworks and developments in multi-agent systems.

The excellent quality of this workshop has been recognized since its inception and its post-proceedings have been regularly published in Springer's Lecture Notes in Artificial Intelligence series. More information about the MABS workshop series may be found at the site http://www.pcs.usp.br/~mabs.

MABS 2011 was hosted at the 10th International Conference on Autonomous Agents and Multi-Agent Systems (AAMAS 2011), which was held in Taipei, Taiwan, during May 2–6, 2011. In this edition, 21 submissions from 14 countries were received, from which we selected 10 for presentation (near 47% acceptance). The papers presented in the workshop have been revised, and eventually extended and reviewed again, in order to make part of this proceedings volume.

We are very grateful to the participants who provided a lively atmosphere of debate during the presentation of the papers and during the general discussion about the challenges that the MABS field faces. We are also very grateful to all the members of the Program Committee and the additional reviewers for their hard work. Thanks are also due to Frank Dignum (AAMAS 2011 Workshop Chair), to Peter Stone and Liz Sonenberg (AAMAS 2011 General Co-chairs), to Kagan Tumer and Pinar Yolum (AAMAS 2011 Program Co-chairs) and to Von-Wun Soo (AAMAS 2011 local organizing Committee Chair).

August 2011

Daniel Villatoro
Jordi Sabater-Mir
Jaime Simão Sichman

Organization

General and Program Chairs

Daniel Villatoro   IIIA-CSIC, Spain
Jordi Sabater-Mir   IIIA-CSIC, Spain
Jaime Simão Sichman   University of São Paulo, Brazil

MABS Steering Committee

Frédéric Amblard   University of Toulouse, France
Jaime Simão Sichman   University of São Paulo, Brazil
Keiki Takadama   University of Electro-Communications, Japan
Keith Sawyer   Washington University in St. Louis, USA
Luis Antunes   University of Lisbon, Portugal
Nigel Gilbert   University of Surrey, UK
Paul Davidsson   Blekinge Institute of Technology, Sweden
Rosaria Conte   National Research Council, Italy
Scott Moss   Manchester Metropolitan University, UK

Program Committee

Armando Geller   George Mason University, USA
Bruce Edmonds   Manchester Metropolitan University, UK
Catholijn Jonker   Delft University of Technology,
                          The Netherlands
Cesareo Hernández Iglesias INSISOC, Valladolid, Spain
Cristiano Castelfranchi ISTC-CNR, Italy
Daniel Villatoro   IIIA-CSIC, Spain (PC Co-chair)
David Sallach   Argonne National Lab and University of
                          Chicago, USA
Diana Adamatti   Federal University of Rio Grande, Brazil
Elizabeth Sklar   City University of New York, USA
Emma Norling   Manchester Metropolitan University, UK
Francisco Grimaldo   Universitat de Valencia, Spain
Frédéric Amblard   University of Toulouse, France
François Bousquet   CIRAD, France
Gennaro Di Tosto   Universiteit Utrecht, The Netherlands
H. Van Parunak   NewVectors LLC, USA
Helder Coelho   Lisbon University, Portugal

Isaac Pinyol	ASCAMM, Spain
Jaime Sichman	University of São Paulo, Brazil (PC Co-chair)
Jean-Pierre Briot	Université Paris 6, France
Jean-Pierre Muller	CIRAD, France
João Balsa	Universidade de Lisboa, Portugal
Jordi Sabater-Mir	IIIA-CSIC, Spain (PC Co-chair)
Joseph Giampapa	Carnegie Mellon University, USA
Juliette Rouchier	Greqam-CNRS, France
Keith Sawyer	Washington University in St. Louis, USA
Keiki Takadama	University of Electro-Communications, Japan
Klaus Troitzsch	University of Koblenz, Germany
Laszlo Gulyas	Aitia International, Inc., Hungary
Maciej Latek	George Mason University, USA
Manuela Veloso	Carnegie Mellon University, USA
Marco Janssen	Indiana University, USA
Mario Paolucci	ISTC-CNR Rome, Italy
Mark Hoogendoorn	Vrije Universiteit Amsterdam, The Netherlands
Michael Lees	NTU, Singapore
Nigel Gilbert	University of Surrey, UK
Nuno David	Lisbon University Institute, ISCTE, Portugal
Oswaldo Teran	University of Los Andes, Venezuela
Pablo Noriega	IIIA-CSIC, Spain
Paul Davidsson	Blekinge Institute of Technology, Sweden
Paulo Novais	Universidade do Minho, Portugal
Rainer Hegselmann	University of Bayreuth, Germany
Riccardo Boero	University of Turin, Italy
Samer Hassan	Universidad Complutense de Madrid, Spain
Shah Jamal Alam	University of Michigan, USA
Tibor Bosse	Vrije Universiteit Amsterdam, The Netherlands
Wander Jager	University of Groningen, The Netherlands

Additional Referees

Eric Guerci	GREQAM-CNRS, France
Inacio Guerberoff	Boston College, USA
Narine Udumyan	GREQAM-CNRS, France

Table of Contents

Agent Simulation of Peer Review: The PR-1 Model

Francisco Grimaldo[1], Mario Paolucci[2], and Rosaria Conte[2]

[1] Departament d'Informàtica
Universitat de València
Av. Vicent Andrés Estellés, s/n, Burjassot, Spain, 46100
francisco.grimaldo@uv.es
[2] Italian National Research Council (CNR)
Institute of Cognitive Sciences and Technologies (ISTC)
Viale Marx 15, Roma, Italy, RM 00137
{mario.paolucci,rosaria.conte}@istc.cnr.it

Abstract. Peer review lies at the core of current scientific research. It is composed of a set of social norms, practices and processes that connect the abstract scientific method with the society of people that apply the method. As a social construct, peer review should be understood by building theory-informed models and comparing them with data collection. Both these activities are evolving in the era of automated computation and communication: new modeling tools and large bodies of data become available to the interested scholar. In this paper, starting from abstract principles, we develop and present a model of the peer review process. We also propose a working implementation of a subset of the general model, developed with Jason, a framework that implements the Belief-Desire-Intention (BDI) model for multi agent systems. After running a set of simulations, varying the initial distribution of reviewer skill, we compare the aggregates that our simplified model produces with recent findings, showing how for some parameter choice the model can generate data in qualitative agreement with measures.

1 Introduction

Science is both a method - a logically coherent set of norms and processes - and a social activity, in which people and organizations endeavour to apply the method. One of the most important elements of the social structure of science is peer review, the process that scrutinizes scientific contributions before they are made available to the community.

As with any social process, peer review should be the object of scientific investigation, and should be evaluated with respect to a set of parameters. Common sense would suggest, at least, considerations of fairness and efficiency. In addition, two specific dimensions very relevant to research are innovation promotion and fraud detection. Science evolves by revolutions [6], and peer review should be evaluated with respect to its reaction to novelty. Is the current system of peer review supporting radical innovation, or is it impeding it?

D. Villatoro, J. Sabater-Mir, and J.S. Sichman (Eds.): MABS 2011, LNAI 7124, pp. 1–14, 2012.

Fraud detection, especially for politically relevant matters as medicine and health, is also extremely important; its actual effectiveness at ensuring quality has yet to be fully investigated. In [7], the review process is found to include a strong "lottery" component, independent of editor and referee integrity. While the multiple review approach to a decision between two options is supported by Condorcet's jury theorem, if we move beyond simple accept/reject decisions by considering scoring and ranking, we find several kinds of potential failures that are not waived by the theorem.

These questions are particularly relevant right now, because, on the one hand, peer review is ready to take advantage of the new information publishing approach created by Web 2.0 and beyond. On the other hand, we perceive a diffuse dissatisfaction of scientists towards the current mechanisms of peer review. This is sometimes testified just anecdotally; list of famous papers that were initially rejected and striking fraudulent cases abound. Leaning on examples is an approach that we do not support because it is known to induce bias [13]. However, some recent papers have shown some numerical evidence on the failures of peer review [4].

In fact, peer review is just a specific case of mutual scoring. Following [9,10], it is a reciprocal and symmetric type of evaluation which includes narrow access and transparency to the target (at least this is how it is designed in the case of teamwork, see the example of scientific research evaluation). Peer review is the standard that journals and granting agencies use to ensure the scientific quality of their publications and funded projects.

The question that follows is then - can we improve on this process? We are not going to fall for the technology trap, and just suggest that by updating peer review to the Web X.0 filtering, tagging, crowdsourcing, and reputation management practices [10], every problem will disappear - in fact, change could make the problems worse; consider for example the well known averaging effect of searching and crowd filtering [3].

Instead, we propose to create a model (or better, a plurality of models) of peer review, that takes into account recent theoretical developments in recommender systems and reputation theories, and test "in silico" the proposed innovations. In this work, we draw an overview of how we foresee such a model, and we present a first, partial implementation of it. Although the literature of simulation models about peer review is scarce, we highlight the results presented in [12], where the authors focus on an optimizing view of the reviewer for his or her own advantage, and those of [8], aimed at encouraging "good" research behaviour by means of the OpinioNet reputation model.

The rest of the paper is organized as follows: the next section outlines a general model of peer review as well as a restricted model focusing on the roles of the reviewer and the conference. Section 3 explains how the latter has been implemented as a Multi-Agent System (MAS) over Jason [2]. In section 4 we show the aggregates that our simplified model produces when varying the distribution of reviewers' ability. Finally, in section 5 we state the conclusions of this work and discuss about future lines of research.

2   Description of the Proposed Model

In this section, we draw the outline of a model of peer review (PR-M in the following) and of its subset that we have implemented. We use agent-based simulation as a modelling technique [1]. With respect to statistical techniques employed for example in [4] or [7], the agent-based or individual-based approach allows us to model the process explicitly. In addition, it helps focusing on agents, their interaction, and possibly also their special roles - consider for example the proposal in [7] of increasing pre-screening of editors or editorial boards. Such a change is based on trust in the fair performance of a few individuals who take up the editors role. Thus, these individuals deserve detailed modeling, that could allow us to reason on their goals and motivations [5].

In this model, we want to catch the whole social process of review, and not just the workings of the single selection process. We will try to simulate the whole lifecycle of peer review, that will allow for example - in the complete model - to reason about role superposition between author and reviewer. This approach distinguishes our effort from that of other authors like [4].

2.1   PR-M

The key entities in our system are: the *paper*, as the basic unit of evaluation; the *author* of the paper; and the *reviewer*, which participate in a program committee of a specific *conference*. We define them in the following paragraphs.

Paper. Here, we do not focus on research but on its evaluation. We assume that the actual value of a paper - that we take as the basic research brick - is difficult to ascertain. While we are aware that this is a strong simplification, we give to each paper a numerical value[1], we speculate that the value is only accessible through a procedure that implies the possibility of mistakes.

As a consequence, value is hidden by noise and evaluating papers is modeled as a difficult task - though, noise can obviously be canceled by repeated independent evaluations. In our model, we give papers an intrinsic fixed value. But there is another, different value that can be calculated and that changes in time: the number of citations that the paper receives.

The value of a paper as the number of its citation should, in an ideal case, reflect its actual value. In PR-M, we plan to implement a citation system so that approved papers can be cited by other papers, thus creating a network of citations. The decision process will be carried on by the simulated author. With both an intrinsic value and a citation count, after an initial bootstrapping phase, we could check the correlation between these two. The larger the correlation, the better the whole system of peer review is performing.

---

[1] How to modify this assumption is an interesting research question. We can imagine creating a vector of quality dimensions as presentation, technical quality, and innovation; and also removing the assumption completely - to a point in which we could say that papers do not exist, but only their interpretation. As a first attempt, and to provide a reference, using a single value seems to be the obvious choice.

Author. Authors create papers and submit them to the conferences. With the citation network, the author will also decide on what papers are to be included in the bibliography. We plan to develop a probabilistic choice where a paper will have a higher chance to be cited depending on a list of factors including paper presence in a conference where the author is in the PC, or has submitted a paper; being co-authored by the author himself; and being a highly cited paper, thus mirroring the positive feedback mechanism that operates in research. Authors could have individual preferences on the weights. By varying the distribution of the intrinsic value of the papers submitted as well as the author preferences, the PR-M model will allow us to analyze the evolution of the quality of the papers published by each conference.

Reviewer. Reviewers can be part of the program committee (PC) of any number of conferences. In every simulation cycle, representing one year or conference edition, they evaluate a certain number of papers for each conference that enlists them in the PC.

The PR-M model characterizes reviewers by a probability value, named reviewer skill (s), that represents the chance they actually understand the paper they are reviewing.

The distribution of s values is the primary cause of reviewing noise. We will experiment with several distributions, including a uniform distribution of s values across reviewers (which we consider a low level of noise in evaluations) and other, left-skewed distributions where a low level of reviewing skill is more frequent.

Conference. As with the paper, we use the term conference in a general sense; it covers also, for example, the journal selection process. The authors' decision about what conference to send their works to is crucial, since the number of papers received is a measure of success for the conference, and their quality will determine the conference's quality. Can the review-conference system ensure quality in the face of very strong noise, variable reviewers skill, thanks to some selection process of PC composition that leans on the simplest measurable quantity - disagreement? The number of evaluations a paper receives are just a few - three being a typical case. Thus, the conference is where all the process comes together - are three reviews enough to cancel noise? For what distributions of papers and reviewers skill?

2.2   PR-1

In this paper, we only present a restricted implementation of the full model. This restricted model, that we call PR-1, contains a subset of the features in PR-M, focusing on the roles of the reviewer and the conference only. Thus, the authors and the papers are not included in the following PR-1 definition.

PR-1 represents the peer review problem by a tuple $\langle R, C \rangle$, where R is the set of *reviewers* participating in the PC of a set of *conferences* C.

Each reviewer $r \in R$ has an associated skill value $s \in [0, 1]$. The result of reviewing is accurate with probability s, and completely random with probability $(1 - s)$. To test different distributions in the unit segment, we use the beta distribution. Depending on its two parameters (see figure 1), this distribution can easily express very diverse shapes such as: a uniform skill distribution ($\alpha = 1, \beta = 1$); a set of moderately low skill reviewers ($\alpha = 2, \beta = 4$), and a mix of very good and very bad reviewers ($\alpha = 0.4, \beta = 0.4$).

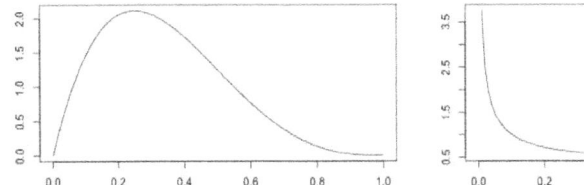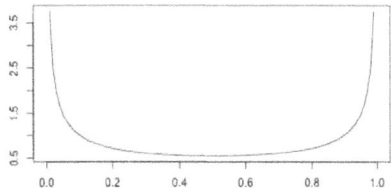

Fig. 1. Beta distributions used in the paper. From left to right, values for (α, β): (2,4) corresponding to low skill reviewers, (0.4, 0.4) corresponding to a mix of very good and very bad reviewers. The uniform distribution, also used in the paper, is not shown.

Conferences $c \in C$ are represented by the tuple:

$$c = \langle np, rp, pr, R_c, pa, ac, I, d, e \rangle$$

Each conference receives a number of papers np every year, and employs a subset of reviewers $R_c \subseteq R$ to prepare rp reviews for each paper. The size of the PC ($|R_c|$) depends on the number of reviews done per PC member pr.

Papers have an associated value representing their intrinsic value, and receive a review value from each reviewer. The intrinsic values follow a uniform distribution over a N-values ordered scale, interpretable as the standard from strong reject to strong accept scores. Conferences accept the best pa papers whose average review value is greater than the acceptance value ac. That is, pa determines the size of the conference measured in terms of the number of papers accepted.

We also introduce a PC update mechanism in the face of disagreement. The purpose here is to test a mechanism that could contribute to improvement of papers quality by removing PC members that disagree with others. While there is no such mechanism currently in operation - at least openly, because PC formation is left in most cases to the arbitrary decisions of chairs - in the era of electronic reputation systems, it is not strange to think of ways to make reviewers, in some sense, accountable.

Thus, after the reviewing process, the conference updates the images $i \in I$ of each reviewer in R, according to the disagreement with the other reviewers of the same paper. This disagreement is calculated for each paper as the difference between the review value given by the reviewer and the average review value for that paper. When this difference gets higher than a disagreement threshold d, the reviewer disagreement count grows by one; values are recorder in an image representation of the form $i = \langle r, nd, nr \rangle$, where r is the reviewer, nd is the accumulated number of disagreements and nr is the total number of reviews carried out. These images are then used to discard the e reviewers with a higher ratio nd/nr and select e new reviewers from R. This way, conferences perform a selection process which selects reviewers who provide similar evaluations. Given our choice for reviewers' mistakes (if they don't understand the paper, the evaluation is random), this mechanism should also select good reviewers.

3 Implementation Details

The PR-1 model has been programmed as a MAS over Jason [2], which allows the definition of BDI agents using an extended version of AgentSpeak(L) [11]. This MAS represents both conferences and reviewers as agents interacting in a common environment. Thus, the PR-1 MAS can be configured to run different simulations and evaluate the effects of the parameters in the PR-1 model. For instance, the code in Table 1 shows how to launch a simulation with 10 conferences and a pool of 500 reviewers.

Table 1. The PR-1 MAS launcher configured for 10 conferences and 500 reviewers

```
1    MAS pr_1
2    {
3          infrastructure: Centralised
4
5          environment: env.PeerReviewEnv(10, 500)
6
7          agents:   conference #10;
8                    reviewer #500;
9
10         aslSourcePath: "asl";
11   }
```

The reviews carried out by the pool of reviewers can be simply programmed in AgentSpeak(L) as shown in Table 2. Here, we use the belief `skill` to set the skill value associated with each reviewer. As already mentioned, we can change the distribution of these values through the (α, β) parameters of a beta distribution (lines 1–3). Each time the reviewer has to review a paper, the `+?review` test plan is executed (lines 6–11). Then, the review is accurate with probability S, and completely random with probability $(1 - S)$.

Conferences can be configured through a set of beliefs in the `conference.asl` file. Table 3 shows the ontology of beliefs used to set parameters such as: the number of papers received (`n_received_papers`), how many of them can be accepted (`max_papers_accepted`) or the number of discordant reviewers that get substituted per year (`n_reviewers_exchanged`). Additionally, a set of `image` beliefs will be managed by each conference in order to represent the images of the

Table 2. `reviewer.asl` file defining the reviewer's behavior

```
1   skill(tools.beta(1,1)).          // Uniform distribution
2   // skill(tools.beta(2,4)).       // Low skill reviewers
3   // skill(tools.beta(0.4,0.4)).   // Polarized reviewer skill
4
5   // Plan to review papers
6   +?review(IdPaper, Value, Review) : skill(S) & paper_scale_values(N)
7      <- if (math.random < S)
8         {
9            Review = Value
10        } else {
11           Review  = math.floor(math.random(N)) + 1
12        }.
```

Table 3. The ontology by the conference agents

Belief formula	Description
n_received_papers(NP)	NP is the amount of papers received by the conference.
reviews_x_paper(RP)	RP is the number of reviews done for each paper.
papers_x_reviewer(PR)	PR is the number of papers reviewed by each reviewer.
max_papers_accepted(PA)	PA is the maximum number of papers the conference accepts.
paper_scale_values(N)	N is the scale of values for the papers.
accept_value(AC)	AC is minimum value for a paper to be accepted.
image(R, ND, NR)	R is the number of the reviewer,
	ND is the accumulated number of disagreements, and
	NR is the number of reviews done by reviewer R.
disagreement_threshold(D)	D is the disagreement threshold to punish reviewers.
n_reviewers_exchanged(E)	E is the number of reviewers exchanged each year.

reviewers in the pool. In addition to the previous beliefs, the `conference.asl` file contains the set of plans dealing with the goals involved in the peer review system. Table 4 shows some snippets of the plans in this file. For instance, the plan `+!celebrateConference` (lines 1–4) first launches the subgoal related to the reviewing process (`!reviewProcess`). For each paper received, a number of RxP reviews are collected (line 11). Then, the conference accepts the best PA papers (lines 30–34) amongst those exceeding the acceptance value AC (lines 13–17). The image of the reviewers in the PC is updated according to the disagreements with the other reviewers of the same paper (lines 19–27). These new images will be used to satisfy the goal of updating the members of the PC (`!updateReviewers`) in line 3.

4   Results

As a proof of concept, in this paper we show what happens in our simplified model (PR-1) if we change the distribution of reviewers' abilities. Thus, we experiment with different initial probability distributions for the only characteristic of reviewers' skill, that is, the probability that a reviewer gets his/her paper right.

Table 4. Plan snippets from the `conference.asl` file

```
1    +!celebrateConference(Year)
2       <- !reviewProcess;
3          !updateReviewers;
4          !!celebrateConference(Year + 1).
5
6    +! reviewProcess : n_received_papers(RP) & reviews_x_paper(RxP) &
7                       accept_value(AC) & max_papers_accepted(PA) &
8                       disagreement_threshold(D) & ...
9       <- for ( .range(PaperId,1,RP) ) {
10           PaperValue = math.floor(math.random(MaxValue)) + 1;
11           for ( .range(I,1, RxP) )  { /* Ask for reviews ... */ }
12           // Evaluate the paper
13           .findall(Review, review(PaperId,_,Review), Reviews);
14           AvgReview = math.average(Reviews);
15           if ( AvgReview > AC ) {
16              +accepted_paper(PaperId, PaperValue, AvgReview);
17           }
18           // Update the image of the reviewers
19           for ( review(PaperId, R, Review) ) {
20              ?image(R, ND, NR);
21              .abolish(image(R,_,_));
22              if (  math.abs(AvgReview - Review) > D  ) {
23                 +image(R, ND+1, NR+1);
24              } else {
25                 +image(R, ND, NR+1);
26              }
27           }
28        }
29        // Limit the number of accepted papers
30        while ( .count(accepted_paper(_,_,_)) > PA ) {
31           .findall(acc_paper(R, PId), acc_paper(PId,_,R), AcceptedPapers);
32           .min(AcceptedPapers, acc_paper(_,PaperIdMin));
33           .abolish(accepted_paper(PaperIdMin,_,_));
34        }.
```

We consider three cases, that is, uniform ability, low average skill, and polarized skill[2]. The shape of the beta distributions that we apply are shown in Fig. 1.

For this first set of experiments, we have ten conferences (which are essentially the same) receiving 100 submissions each (np), drawn from a uniform distribution. Papers are assigned an intrinsic value in a 10-values ordered scale, interpretable as the standard from strong reject to enthusiastically accept scores. We have fixed $pa = 100$ and $ac = 5.5$, so that all papers whose average review value is greater than 5 are accepted. We have set $rp = pr = 3$, i.e., the same number of reviews per paper and per PC member. Thus, a conference will need as many reviewers as it receives papers. That is, conferences will employ 100 reviewers each from a pool of 500 reviewers. There is no limit to PC memberships for an individual reviewer. Ideally, the same group of 100 reviewers could constitute the PC of all ten conferences. Finally, we use a disagreement threshold of 4 (d) and a 10% reviewer turnover rate($e = 10$). Substitute reviewers are selected randomly in the pool.

---

[2] High average skill is not considered because the uniform distribution already yields a high quality selection process.

4.1   Measured Quantities

For each set of experiments, we measure several quantities, that we present, in their time evolution, in the following figures. The results are presented with five number summary (the central line marks the median, then the successive quartiles), collecting together the data of the different conferences (that are equivalent in PR-1) and in a window of five consecutive years.

The average accepted quality is the primary measure of success for the selection system. Paper quality, if the review process works perfectly, should select 20 top score papers, 20 with quality 9, and 10 of quality 8, leading to an ideal score of 9.2. The worst possible case (papers are accepted completely at random), as a reference value, would simply be the mean of scores from one to ten, amounting to 5.5.

In parallel to the paper selection process, based on disagreement measures between reviewers, program committees are reorganized with the aim to select the best reviewers. Thus, another quantity we measure is the average quality of reviewers that are part of program committees, under different initial conditions for their distribution. In principle, better reviewers should select better papers.

We also show the number of good papers (i.e., with an intrinsic value greater than 5.5) rejected, and the number of bad papers (i.e., with an intrinsic value less than 5.5) accepted. While the previous quantities can be seen as measures of efficiency, these two can be thought of as measures of fairness.

In fact, good papers rejected and bad papers accepted are especially important because of the high-stakes nature of investment that researchers do on each paper - on the one hand, an "out-of-the-blue" rejection can seriously impact career, especially in small research groups; on the other hand, the publication of bogus papers creates a stigma on journals and conferences. Finally, another interesting measure of success for a conference review process had been defined in [4] as *divergence*: the normalized distance between the ordering of the accepted papers, and the ordering induced by another quality measure.

In [4], divergence was calculated with real data of an anonymised "large conference", comparing review results against paper citation rates registered five years later. We perform a similar calculation, not against citation rates but against our idealized paper quality. The distance used is calculated simply by the (normalized) number of elements ranked in the top (1/3 or 2/3) by the review process that are not in the top (1/3 or 2/3) in the ideal quality ordering. The result for the large conference, that the authors of [4] claim to be disappointingly comparable to random sorting, is a value of 0.63 at 1/3 and 0.32 at 2/3.

Note how this ordering concerns only the set of accepted papers; good rejected papers or bad accepted ones do not enter this calculation. This value can be considered as another measure of efficiency of the system: the lower it is, the more efficient the peer review.

4.2 Uniform Ability

Here we show the results obtained from a reviewer skill distribution with parameters (1,1) - a uniform distribution.

From figure 2, we can see how the quality of accepted papers starts already over the average. The process improves in time for both the paper quality and reviewer skill; however, only the second has a significant effect. The convergence process seems to manage selecting good reviewers, but this happens without a substantial quality improvement. Mistakes in paper evaluations show only a slight decrease. Finally, divergence from the optimal acceptance ordering remains constant - perhaps after a slight improvement in the first years. At about 0.28 and 0.2, it remains far better than the levels 0.63 and 0.32 reported in [4].

4.3 Low Average Skill

Apparently, our simulated reviewers perform better than the real ones. What if we decrease their average skill, for example drawing them from a beta distribution with parameters (2.0, 4.0), shown in figure 1 (left)? The results are presented in figure 3. With such a bad average reviewer skill, the quality of accepted papers results lower than in the previous case, and the agreement process yields no or little improvement in time - except in reviewers skill, whose increase however does not seem enough to improve the quality of accepted papers. There just aren't enough good reviewers around to make the process work. Good papers rejected and bad papers accepted abound, making up for more than half the body of accepted papers; divergence, ending at 0.6 and 0.25, seems directly comparable to the values in [4].

4.4 Polarized Skill

So fare we have shown a relatively good selection process, starting with reviewers with uniform distribution, and a relatively bad one, where most reviewers are of low skill. With yet another shape of the skill distribution, we want to measure how effective the agreement process is in selecting good reviewers. To this purpose, we choose an initial distribution with a double peak - in this experiment, as can be seen from figure 1 (right), most reviewers are very bad or very good. We surely have more than enough good ones for a nearly perfect review process - but will the system be able to select them? Figure 4 shows this is indeed the case. This time, the success of the reviewer selection process takes the average paper quality up with it, obtaining better results than in the uniform case. There are nearly no bad papers accepted, nor good papers rejected towards the end. Divergence is similarly affected, leveling at 0.2 and 0.12 at the end.

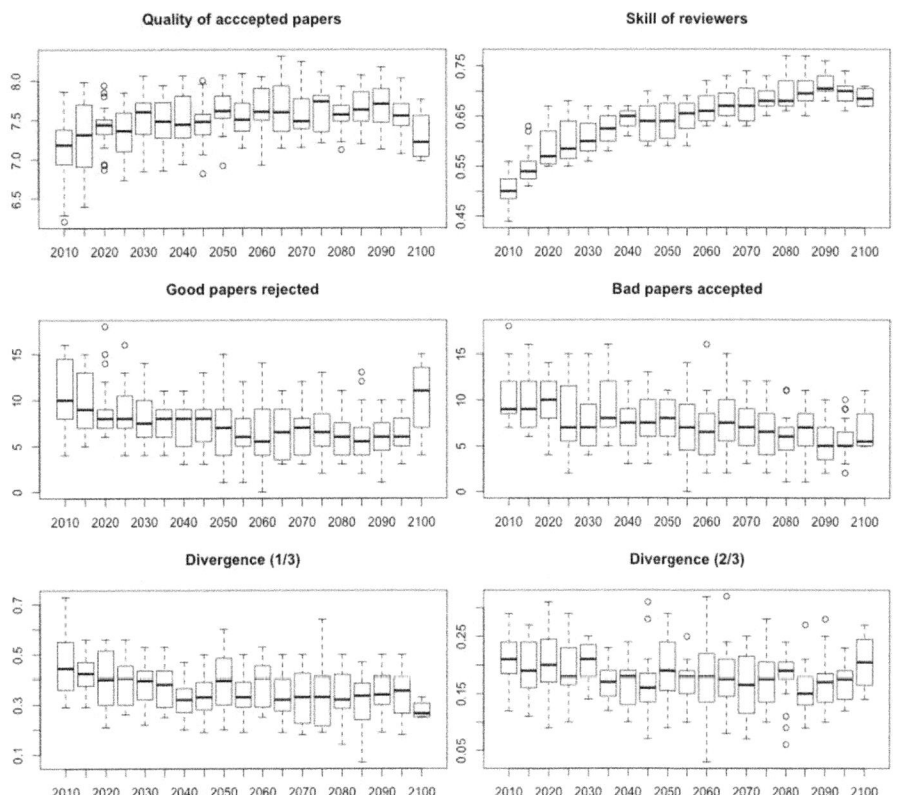

Fig. 2. Results (shown as five-number summary) for a beta distribution with parameters (*1.0*, *1.0*), that is, a uniform distribution, averaged over ten conferences and in periods of five years. *First row*, left, average quality of accepted papers; right, quality of reviewers. Both observable quantities improve substantially in time. *Second row*, left, good papers rejected, right, bad papers accepted, both showing a small improvement in time. *Third row*, divergence values calculated at 1/3 and 2/3, both decreasing in time.

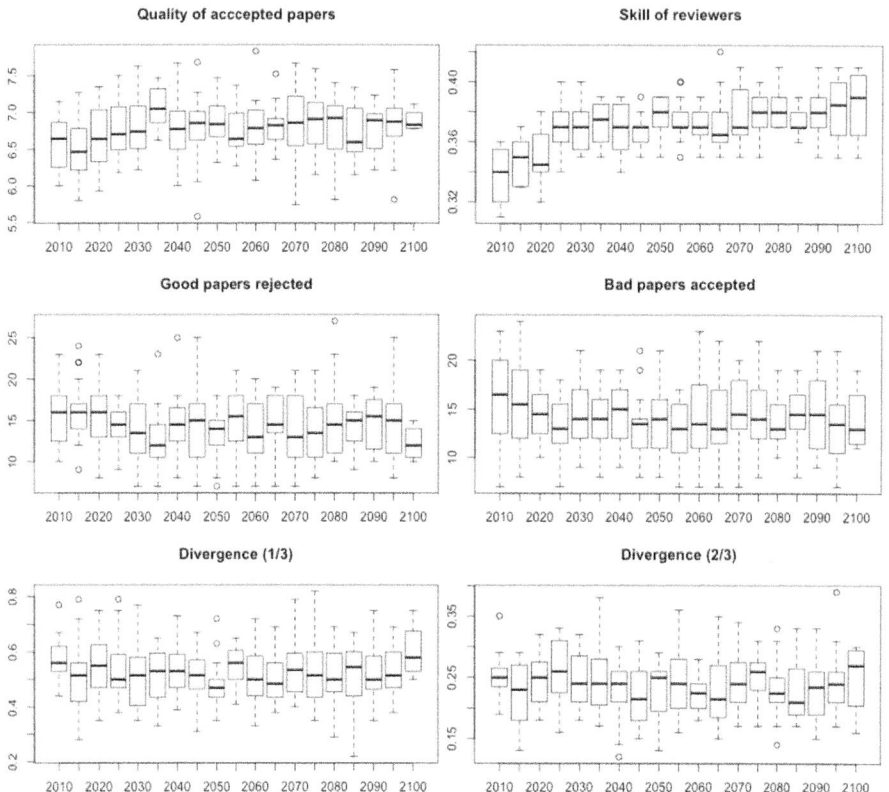

Fig. 3. Results (shown as five-number summary) for a beta distribution with parameters (*2.0, 4.0*), averaged over ten conferences and in periods of five years. *First row*, left, average quality of accepted papers; right, quality of reviewers. There is no substantial improvement, apart from an increase in reviewers quality. *Second row*, left, good papers rejected, right, bad papers accepted, both stable in time. *Third row*, divergence values calculated at 1/3 and 2/3.

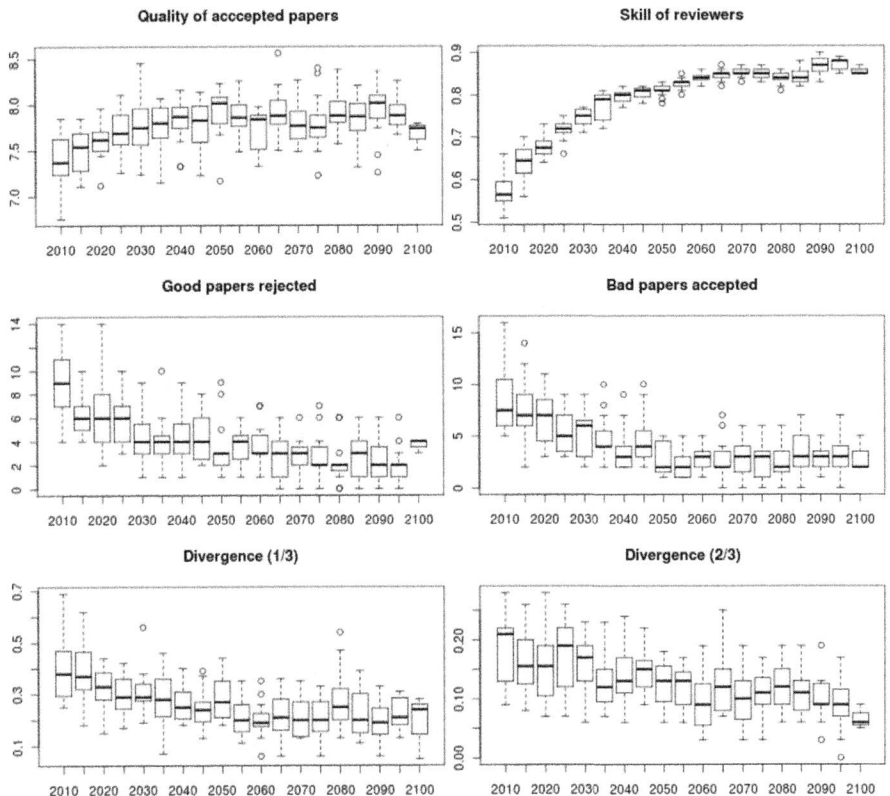

Fig. 4. Results (shown as five-number summary) for a beta distribution with parameters $(0.4, 0.4)$, averaged over ten conferences and in periods of five years. *First row*, left, average quality of accepted papers; right, quality of reviewers. Both observable quantities improve substantially in time. *Second row*, left, good papers rejected, right, bad papers accepted. Both show a marked decrease in time. *Third row*, divergence values calculated at $1/3$ and $2/3$, both decreasing in time.

5   Discussion and Future Work

This paper is a first step towards a model of peer review devoted to study and to enhance the way of evaluating scientific research. We have sketched the main elements involved as well as the relations amongst them. A first restricted version of the full model, that we call PR-1, has been implemented as a MAS over Jason. The results show how a conference review process based on disagreement control between reviewers can i) improve in time both the quality of accepted papers and the reviewer skill of PC members; ii) reduce the number of good papers rejected and bad papers accepted; and iii) lower the divergence between the ordering of the accepted papers and an ideal quality ordering. Reviewer selection improves on both the efficiency and the fairness of the review process. The results, for what regards a measure of divergence between reviews and actual quality of the paper, are shown to be qualitatively comparable with the observed data in [4].

Quite a large number of issues still remain open for future work. Limiting PC memberships for individual reviewers and considering role superposition between author and reviewer is one of the next steps. Subsequent versions of the PR model should include the active role of the authors when deciding which conference to send their works to, as it can vary the distribution of the papers submitted to a conference. Furthermore, statistical data coming from conference management systems must be used to validate the results provided by the model.

Acknowledgements. This work was supported by the Spanish MICINN, Consolider Programme and Plan E funds, as well as European Commission FEDER funds, under Grants CSD2006-00046 and TIN2009-14475-C04-04. It was also partly supported by the Spanish MEC under grant JC2010-0062.

References

1. Bonabeau, E.: Agent-based modeling: methods and techniques for simulating human systems. Proceedings of the National Academy of Sciences of the United States of America 99(suppl. 3), 7280–7287 (2002)
2. Bordini, R.H., Hübner, J.F.: Jason (March 2007), http://jason.sourceforge.net/
3. Brabazon, T.: The google effect: Googling, blogging, wikis and the flattening of expertise. Libri 56, 157–167 (2006)
4. Casati, F., Marchese, M., Ragone, A., Turrini, M.: Is peer review any good? a quantitative analysis of peer review. Technical report, Ingegneria e Scienza dell'Informazione, University of Trento (2009)
5. Conte, R., Castelfranchi, C.: Cognitive Social Action. UCL Press, London (1995)
6. Kuhn, T.S.: The Structure of Scientific Revolutions, 3rd edn. University of Chicago Press (December 1996)
7. Neff, B.D., Olden, J.D.: Is peer review a game of chance? BioScience 56(4), 333–340 (2006)
8. Osman, N., Sabater, J., Sierra, C.: Simulating research behaviour (this volume)
9. Paolucci, M., Balke, T., Conte, R., Eymann, T., Marmo, S.: Review of internet user-oriented reputation applications and application layer networks. Social Science Research Network Working Paper Series (September 2009)
10. Paolucci, M., Picascia, S., Marmo, S.: Electronic reputation systems. In: Handbook of Research on Web 2.0, 3.0, and X.0, ch. 23, pp. 411–429. IGI Global (2010)
11. Rao, A.S.: AgentSpeak(L): BDI Agents Speak Out in a Logical Computable Language. In: Perram, J., Van de Velde, W. (eds.) MAAMAW 1996. LNCS (LNAI), vol. 1038, pp. 42–55. Springer, Heidelberg (1996)
12. Thurner, S., Hanel, R.: Peer-review in a world with rational scientists: Toward selection of the average (August 2010)
13. Wainberg, J., Kida, T., Smith, J.F.: Stories vs. statistics: The impact of anecdotal data on accounting decision making. Social Science Research Network Working Paper Series (March 2010)

Simulating Research Behaviour

Nardine Osman, Jordi Sabater-Mir, Carles Sierra, and Jordi Madrenas-Ciurana

Artificial Intelligence Research Institute (IIIA-CSIC), Barcelona, Catalonia, Spain
{nardine,jsabater,sierra,jmadrenas}@iiia.csic.es

Abstract. This paper presents a simulation of research behaviour, focusing on the process of writing papers, submitting them to journals and conferences, reviewing them, and accepting/rejecting them. The simulation is currently used to evaluate the OpinioNet reputation model, which calculates the reputation of researchers and research work based on the propagation of opinions amongst related entities. The goal is to verify whether the reputation model succeeds in encouraging 'good' research behaviour or not, although the simulator is elaborate enough to be used for the analysis of other aspects of paper writing, submission, and review processes.

1   Introduction

The classical way in which scientific publications are produced, evaluated and credited, is being challenged by the use of modern computer science technologies [1,4]. In particular, software versioning tools and reputation mechanisms make it realistic to think about a publication process where the publications are 'liquid', in the sense that they are persistently accessible over Internet and modified along time. Credit is then given to authors based on opinions, reviews, comments, etc. This would produce many beneficial results, for instance, to re duce the current large number of very similar publications (i.e. salami papers) or to organise conferences by just searching for the most prestigious liquid publications satisfying certain keywords. OpinioNet [3] is one reputation model that has been proposed with the intent of encouraging 'good' research behaviour. For instance, its equations are designed to give more attention to the quality of a researcher's work than their quantity.

This paper proposes a simulator that would simulate the course of scientific publications, from writing papers and submitting them to journals and conferences to reviewing them and accepting/rejecting them. The main goal is to verify whether the OpinioNet reputation model succeeds in encouraging 'good' research behaviour or not, although the simulator is rich enough to be used for the analysis of other aspects of paper writing, submission, and review processes.

The rest of this paper is divided as follows. Section 2 provides the background needed for understanding the followed formal publications model and the OpinioNet reputation model being evaluated. Section 3 introduces the basics of the simulator. The simulator's algorithm is then presented by Sect. 4, and its assumptions and hypothesis are presented by Sect. 5. Section 6 then discusses some results, before concluding with Sect. 7.

D. Villatoro, J. Sabater-Mir, and J.S. Sichman (Eds.): MABS 2011, LNAI 7124, pp. 15–30, 2012.

2   Background

Reputation is widely understood as a group's opinion about the entity in question. The OpinioNet reputation model [3] is based on the concept that in the case of the lack of explicit opinions, opinions may be deduced from related entities. For instance, in the field of publications, one may assume that if a paper has been accepted by a reputable conference, then the paper should be of a minimum quality. Similarly, a conference becomes reputable if it accepts high quality papers. OpinioNet is essentially based on this notion of opinion propagation in structural graphs, such as the publications graphs (where nodes of this graph may represent knowledge objects, such as conference proceedings and conference papers, and relations state which node is part of which other).

OpinioNet understands opinions as probability distributions over an evaluation space (such as $\{poor, good, v.good, excellent\}$), for a particular attribute (such as novelty of work), and at a moment in time. OpinioNet then defines the structural graph accordingly: $SG = \langle N, G, O, E, A, T, \mathcal{E}, \mathcal{F} \rangle$, where N is the set of nodes, G is the set of researchers that may generate opinions about nodes, O is the set of all opinions that researchers may hold, E is the ordered evaluation space for O (e.g. $E = \{poor, good, v.good, excellent\}$), A is the set of attributes that opinions may address (for instance, $A = \{novelty, clarity, significance, correctness\}$), T represents calendar time, $\mathcal{E} \subseteq N \times N$ specifies which nodes are part of the structure of which others (i.e. $(n, n') \in \mathcal{E}$ implies n is part of n'), $\mathcal{F} : G \times N \times A \times T \to O$ is a relation that links a given researcher, node, attribute, and time to their corresponding opinion.

A single opinion is then represented as the probability distribution $\mathbb{P}(E|G, N, A, T) \in O$. We note that probability distributions subsume classical approaches and are more informative. Hence, the adoption of this approach by our simulator does not necessarily restrict its application to other scenarios (and translation between different reputation measures, including probability distributions, is presented by [6,3,2]).

3   Simulation Basics

In theory, it is researchers' behaviour (defined through their profiles) that would influence the creation and evolution of papers, journals, and, eventually, fields of research. However, to keep the simulation simple, our example focuses on the evolution of one specific aspect of a research community — namely, the growth of the community's contributions — and neglects other aspects that are not deemed crucial for the evaluation of the reputation module — such as the rise and fall of the community itself, its journals, its fields of research, etc. As such, and for the sake of simplifying the simulation, we choose to simulate a single community with a fixed number of researchers researching a given subject; we say it is the researchers' profiles that control the production and dissemination of single contributions; and we keep the number of journals that could accept/reject these contributions fixed. In other words, we say one 'top rated' journal is sufficient to represent the acceptance of a contribution by *any* 'top rated' journal. We argue that since our current interest is in the future of authors' contributions (such as papers or book chapters), the number of journals becomes irrelevant: what is crucial is the quality of the journals (if any) that accept the authors' contributions. In what follows, we define the simulator's input and output, followed by the journals' and researchers' profiles that define their behaviour.

3.1   The Simulator's Input and Output

The simulator requires the following tuple as input: $\langle SG^0, J, U, \mathcal{J}, \mathcal{U}, \mathbf{T} \rangle$, where SG^0 describes the initial state of the system (or the initial SG graph), which should include at least a fixed number of researchers and journals; J describes the set of journal profiles (defined shortly); U describes the set of researcher profiles (defined shortly); $\mathcal{J} \subseteq N \times J$ is a function that maps a journal in N (where N is the set of knowledge objects in SG^0) to a journal profile in J; $\mathcal{U} \subseteq G \times U$ is a function that maps a researcher in G (where G is the set of researchers in SG^0) to a researcher profile in U; and $\mathbf{T} \in \mathbb{N}^*$ describes the number of years to be simulated. Then, every simulation year Y results in a modified structural graph SG^Y. The evolution of the SG graph is then presented as $E_{SG} = \{SG^0, \cdots, SG^{\mathbf{T}}\}$.

3.2   Journals' Profiles

Journals are categorised through profiles that define their quality and their required number of reviewers. A journal's profile $j \in J$ is defined as the tuple: $j = \langle \mathbb{J}, \mathbf{RN} \rangle$, where similar to the opinions on quality, $\mathbb{J}$ is a probability distribution over the evaluation space E describing the quality of the journal;[1] and $\mathbf{RN}$ describes the number of reviewers needed to review a paper, and it is specified as a Gaussian function over the set of natural numbers $\mathbb{N}$.

The rules for accepting/rejecting contributions depends on the quality of the journal $\mathbb{J}$. For example, very good journals are very strict about the quality of the papers they accept, other lower quality ones are not as strict. Hence, a journal's acceptance threshold $\mathbf{AT}$ may be defined in terms of its quality $\mathbb{J}$. A preliminary definition could be to have $\mathbf{AT} = emd(\mathbb{J}, \mathbb{T})$, where $\mathbb{T} = \{e_n \mapsto 1\}$ (where $\forall e_i \in E \cdot e_n > e_i$) describes the ideal distribution, or the best quality possible, and emd is the earth movers distance that calculates the distance (whose range is $[0, 1]$, where 0 represents the minimum distance and 1 represents the maximum possible distance) between two probability distributions [5].[2]

---

[1] Just like an opinion describing the quality of a research work is specified as a probability distribution (see Sect. 2), the measure describing the quality of journals is also specified as a probability distribution, providing a richer representation that may easily be translated to more common measures [6,3,2].

[2] If probability distributions are viewed as piles of dirt, then the earth mover's distance measures the minimum *cost* for transforming one pile into the other. This cost is equivalent to the 'amount of dirt' times the distance by which it is moved, or the distance between elements of the ordered evaluation space E.

3.3   Researchers' Profiles

Similar to journals, researchers' behaviour is also categorised through profiles that define their quality, their productivity, etc. A researcher's profile $u \in U$ is defined as the tuple $u = \langle \mathbb{Q}, \mathbf{RP}, \mathbf{CN}, \mathbb{C}, \mathbf{CA}, \mathbf{CP}, \mathbf{SS}, \mathbf{RvP}, \mathbf{RV}, \mathbf{RT} \rangle$, where:

- $\mathbb{Q}$ describes the researcher's research quality, and it is specified as a probability distribution over the evaluation space E (we assume that researchers have a fixed and 'intrinsic' quality of research — Sect. 5 argues the need for this intrinsic value — which is different from reputation values that reflect the view of the community and are calculated by reputation algorithms);
- $\mathbf{RP}$ describes the research productivity in terms of the produced number of papers per year (since produced research work is usually presented and preserved through papers, whether published or unpublished), and it is specified as a Gaussian function over the set of natural numbers $\mathbb{N}$;
- $\mathbf{CN}$ describes the researcher's usual number of coauthors per contribution, and it is specified as a Gaussian function over the set of natural numbers $\mathbb{N}$;
- $\mathbb{C}$ describes the accepted research quality of coauthors, and it is specified as a probability distribution over the evaluation space E;
- $\mathbf{CA}$ describes the accepted affinity level of coauthors (currently, affinity measure describes how close are two researchers' profiles; however, in future simulations, one may also consider affinity measures that describe how close are two researchers with respect to numerous social relations), and the range of its value is the interval $[0, 1]$, where the value 0 represents minimum affinity and the value 1 represents maximum affinity;
- $\mathbf{CP}$ describes the level of persistency in sticking with old coauthors, it is defined in terms of the number of past papers that two researchers have coauthored together, and it is specified as a Gaussian function over the set of natural numbers $\mathbb{N}$;
- $\mathbf{SS}$ describes the submission strategy of the researcher, and the range of its value is the interval $[-1, +1]$, where a value -1 represents an extreme 'risk-averse' strategy in which the researcher does not submit a paper to any journal unless its paper is of the highest quality possible, a value of $+1$ represents an extreme 'risk-seeking' strategy in which the researcher doesn't mind submitting a paper to a journal of much higher quality, and the value 0 represents a more neutral approach in which the researcher usually submits its papers to journals of the same quality (of course, values in between represent different levels of risk-averse and risk-seeking strategies);[3]
- $\mathbf{RvP}$ describes the researcher's review productivity in terms of the number of papers the researcher accepts to review per year, and it is specified as a Gaussian function over the set of natural numbers $\mathbb{N}$;

---

[3] We assume that the quality of journals and that of researchers may be compared since they are measured on the same scale. Our assumption is based on the idea that the quality of the researchers, their papers, and the journals that accept those papers are all based on the quality of the research work being carried out and presented.

- **RV** describes the review quality in terms of how close the researcher's reviews are from the true quality of the papers in question, it is defined in terms of the distance from the true quality of the paper in question, and the range of this distance is the interval $[-1, +1]$; and
- **RT** describes the reviewers' threshold for accepting to review a paper for a given journal, it is defined in terms of the earth mover's distance between the reviewer's quality of research and that of the journal's, and the range of its value is the interval $[0, 1]$.

We note that although the researchers' profiles may seem too complex, many ideas have already been overly simplified (as illustrated by Sect. 5.1), and additional simplifications are straightforward (if needed).

4   Simulation Algorithm

While the previous section has introduced the simulator as a black box, this section presents an overview of the simulation algorithm. (For the simulator's technical details, we refer the interested reader to our technical document [2].) The algorithm's steps are outlined below.

1. *Generate the groups of coauthors for the given year.*
   The idea is that each group of coauthors will produce one paper that will then be added to the *SG* graph. In summary, the algorithm selects the authors one by one, giving the authors that intend to write more papers this year (specified by the research productivity **RP** of the researcher) a higher probability of being selected first. Then, for each selected author, the algorithm searches, in an iterated manner, for a suitable group of coauthors, where 'suitability' is based on the restrictions imposed by each researcher through its preferred number of coauthors (**CN**), the accepted quality of coauthors ($\mathbb{C}$), the accepted affinity of coauthors (**CA**), and the accepted persistency of coauthors (**CP**). The algorithm iterates until all researchers are assigned to as many coalitions as needed.
2. Then, for each paper resulting from a created group of coauthors, the simulator performs the following:
   (a) *Calculate the intrinsic quality of the paper.*
   We base our simulation on the idea that papers have a true quality that researchers (or reviewers) often try to guess. Of course, in reality, this value does not exist (and if it did, it definitely would not be static, but a continuously evolving one). However, simulation may assume such values to compare and analyse the performance of researchers. We assume that when researchers from various qualities (where a researcher's true quality is specified by the parameter $\mathbb{Q}$) are grouped together then the resulting paper's true value would be based on the researchers' true value. How a paper's intrinsic quality is calculated is illustrated shortly by (1).

(b) *Choose the journal to submit the paper to.*

After a paper is created, it is submitted to some journal. The selection of the journal assumes that researchers tend to have certain submission strategies (specified through the parameter **SS**), and the submission strategy for a given journal is an aggregation of its authors'.[4] The calculated submission strategy of a paper is then used to help select the journal to submit the paper to by enforcing constraints on the distance between the paper's true quality (calculated by step 2(a) above) and that of the journal's ($\mathbb{J}$).

(c) *Choose the reviewers to review the paper.*

This action is based on the number of reviews needed **RN**, the availability of the reviewers (researchers are assumed to review a certain number of papers per year, determined by **RvP**, and they accept the journals' requests to review papers based on a first come first serve basis), the quality of the researcher $\mathbb{Q}$, the quality of the journal $\mathbb{J}$, and the reviewer's threshold for accepting a journal (**RT**).

(d) *Generate the reviewers' opinions (reviews) about the paper in question.*

Reviewers' opinions are based on the intrinsic quality of the paper (calculated by step 2(a) above) and the researcher's review quality (**RV**), which determines how close the review would be to the paper's true value.

(e) *Accept/Reject the paper by the chosen journal.*

This calculation is based on the quality of the journal $\mathbb{J}$, the journal's acceptance threshold (**AT**), and the reviewers' aggregated opinions, where the aggregation takes into consideration the reviewers' reputation at the time for weighing each opinion accordingly. Note that if the paper is accepted, then it is linked in the *SG* graph to the journal through the *part of* relation.

(f) *Reputation measures are calculated by OpinioNet.*

After reviews are created and papers are accepted/rejected accordingly, the simulator calls the OpinioNet reputation model to calculate the reputation of papers based on the new reviews and acceptance results, as well as to calculate the authors' reputation based on the reputation of their papers.

3. *Repeat the entire process for the following year.*

Note that the algorithm terminates after simulating a pre-defined number of years, or time-steps, **T**.

Due to space limitations, we suffice with the presented general overview of the simulation algorithm. However, for further technical details, we refer the interested reader to Algorithms 3–8 of our technical document [2].

---

[4] Although, in fields that are known to have an enormous number of authors per paper (for example, it is not uncommon for Physics articles to have a few thousand authors each) and by the law of large numbers, the simple aggregation method of the authors' **SS** values would fail since it would result in similar values for all papers. In such cases, it might be useful to calculate the resulting submission strategy by adopting it from the leading author.

5   Assumptions and Hypotheses

After introducing the proposed simulation algorithm, and before moving on to the experiments and results, this section is intended to clarify our stance by highlighting and discussing the assumptions we make as well as clarifying the claims the simulation algorithm is designed to test.

5.1   Assumptions

As discussed earlier, trying to simulate the actual behaviour of researchers requires a thorough study of various aspects, from how people choose their coauthors and how they choose where to submit their work to, to how do journals select reviewers, and how is the quality of a paper related to the research quality of its authors. We argue that the proposed simulation algorithm is sophisticated enough to capture the actions that have an impact on reputation measures (such as calculating the true quality of papers), yet it is simplified enough to overlook unnecessary complicated behaviour (such as representing all good quality journals as one). As a result, a bunch of assumptions are made, which we discuss below. We note that many of the fixed values that we refer to in our assumptions are in fact either drawn from a predefined Gaussian function, or some noise is added to them to make our scenarios more realistic.

On the Static Nature of the Research Community. We say both the community and the researchers' behaviour are static: researchers do not join or leave the community; journals do not evolve or die; the field of research is fixed; each paper cites a fixed number of other papers; a researcher's productivity does not change with time; a researcher's quality of research does not evolve with time; a researcher's review productivity does not evolve with time; a researcher's review quality does not evolve with time and his reviews always fall at a fixed distance from that of the true quality of the paper being reviewed; a researcher's submission strategy does not evolve with time; a researcher's acceptable journal quality for reviewing papers is fixed; and journals do not evolve and they always accept papers of the same quality.

These assumptions are introduced to keep the simulation simple. We postpone the study of dynamic and evolving behaviour for future work. However, to keep the simulation more realistic, recall that some randomness is introduced when generating the measures specifying a 'fixed' (or 'static') behaviour.

On Selecting Coauthors. Selecting the coauthors to collaborate with is usually a complex matter that depends on a variety of issues, such as the subject of study, the practicality of collaboration, and so on. Our proposed simulator, however, is not aimed at studying the dynamics of human relations, their collaboration, and coalition formations, but the production of papers on an annual basis. Hence, for simplicity, the production of papers assumes researchers produce a fixed number of papers per year, and coauthor their papers with a group of other researchers. Again, for simplicity, we assume the strategy of selecting coauthors is 'fixed' and that coauthors are selected based on their quality, their affinity, and their persistence. Of course, different weights may be given to each.

On the True Quality of Researchers and Research Work. Although in reality the true quality of a researcher is neither definite nor accessible, we do assume that researchers have defined true and fixed qualities. The notion of a 'true' quality value of researchers has some ground in real life. For instance, some behaviour (such as looking for future collaborators, selecting who to give a funding to, etc.) assumes researchers to be of a certain quality, and their research work to follow that quality respectively. We also believe a good reviewer is one that can be as objective as possible by assessing the 'true' quality of the paper (whatever that may mean) free from any biases. Following in those footsteps, the proposed simulation states that the true quality of a paper is based on the true quality of its authors, and the review quality of a researcher depends on how close his opinions are to the true quality of the paper in question.

But how is the true quality of the paper calculated? We say when researchers from various qualities are grouped together then the resulting paper's true (quality) value would be based on the researchers' true (quality) values. However, we also assume that in the worst case scenario, the quality of a research work adopts the quality of the best coauthor. In the best case scenario, when coauthors are all of very good quality, the quality of a research work follow a more superadditive nature. In other words, when very good quality coauthors work together, they can produce work of higher quality compared to what each coauthor can produce on their own. In other words, the effect that a single researcher has on the true quality of a paper is dependent on its quality of coauthors. The equation we propose for calculating a paper's true value $\mathbb{X}$ is then:

$$\mathbb{X} = \begin{cases} \hat{\mathbb{Q}} & \text{, if } \bar{q} > 0.5 \\ (2\bar{q})^\alpha \cdot \hat{\mathbb{Q}} + (1 - (2\bar{q})^\alpha) \cdot \mathbb{T} & \text{, otherwise} \end{cases} \tag{1}$$

where, $\hat{\mathbb{Q}}$ represents the highest quality in the list of the true qualities of the coauthors $\{\mathbb{Q}_{a_1}, \cdots, \mathbb{Q}_{a_n}\}$, $\mathbb{T} = \{e_n \mapsto 1\}$ (where $\forall e_i \in E \cdot e_n > e_i$) describes the best quality possible, $\bar{q}$ represents the mean of the coauthors' qualities $\{q_{a_1}, \cdots, q_{a_n}\}$ (where $q_{a_i} = emd(\mathbb{Q}_{a_i}, \mathbb{T})$), and α is a tuning factor.[5]

In summary, the above equation states that when the average quality of coauthors is low (i.e. $0.5 < \bar{q} \leq 1$), then the quality of the paper adopts the quality of the best coauthor ($\hat{\mathbb{Q}}$). However, when the average quality of coauthors is high (i.e. $0 \leq \bar{q} \leq 0.5$), then the quality of the paper follows a superadditive function that increases the quality of the best coauthor ($\hat{\mathbb{Q}}$) towards the best quality possible ($\mathbb{T}$), based on the average quality of the authors ($\bar{q}$) and a tuning factor (α).

---

[5] It is not clear yet whether the proposed approach for calculating a paper's true values would provide better results than a simple variance of authors' quality values. Future extensive simulations could also clarify which choices are better.

On Selecting the Journal to Submit a Paper to. We say researchers have different, and 'fixed', submission strategies. We define submission strategies following the prospect theory classification of strategies into risk seeking, risk averse, and risk neutral ones. The submission strategy of a paper is then an aggregation of its authors'. For example, if the submission strategy is 'risk seeking', then the paper may be submitted to some journal which is of better quality. If the submission strategy is 'risk averse', then the paper cannot be submitted to a journal unless it is of higher quality. Of course, varying levels of these strategies are considered.

On Selecting Reviewers. Journals usually try to get good reviewers, based on availability. But how do reviewers choose whether to accept/reject reviewing papers for a given journal? We assume that reviewers accept journals based on a first come first serve basis, as long as the journal is of acceptable quality and the reviewer is available to do more reviews.

On Accepting/Rejecting Papers by a Given Journal. We assume accepting/rejecting a paper is only based on reviewers' opinions, and not on the number of papers submitted, the acceptance rate, etc. This is necessary because we have already assumed the number of journals to be fixed. In other words, we say one journal of a given quality is enough to represent all potential journals of that same quality.

Furthermore, when accepting/rejecting a paper, the journal's editors do not base their decision on the true quality of the paper (since this information is not available), but on the aggregated reviewers' opinions. When aggregating reviewers' opinions, we say that the reliability of a review (or opinion) is based on the researcher's current reputation in his/her community (as calculated by the OpinioNet algorithm), rather than how confident he claims to be (which is how the current review process works). We believe this is a stronger reliability measure since the reviewer does not assess himself, but is assessed by the community.

On the Fate of Papers. Finally, we say that, for the sake of simplicity, both accepted and rejected papers are forgotten. Neither of them is submitted to other journals in the following years; only new papers are created each year. In practice these new papers would in fact be a modification of (i.e. a new version of) already existing ones. However, we currently postpone the simulation of the *version of* relation that links related papers for future simulations. This assumption is acceptable since the current simulation simply focuses on the number of papers accepted by journals and the quality of the journals that accept them, rather than the *evolution* of papers.

5.2 Hypotheses

The OpinioNet reputation model has been used in an attempt to encourage 'good' research behaviour [2]. The proposed simulator aims at verifying whether OpinioNet achieves its goal or not through testing the following hypotheses.

Hypothesis 1. *The better the quality of the researcher, the less susceptible they are to the quality of their coauthors.*

Hypothesis 2. *It is more profitable to follow a risk-neutral submission strategy.*

Hypothesis 3. *It is more profitable to produce few high quality papers than several lower quality ones.*

The first hypothesis implies that established top researchers can afford to work with lower quality researchers (such as new PhD students) and still maintain their reputation. However, lower quality researchers are better off collaborating with researchers that are of better quality than themselves in order to increase the quality of their papers, and hence, their reputation (recall that a researcher's true intrinsic quality remains fixed in our simulation). Naturally, this hypothesis is highly influenced by our assumption that the quality of a research work is equal or greater than the quality of the best author. In any case, this issue is revisited when discussing the results of the simulation testing this hypothesis.

The second hypothesis implies that it is more profitable, in terms of reputation, to submit one's contributions to journals that lie in the same quality range of the paper. For instance, if authors choose journals that are much better, then they end up wasting the community's time and resources, and they also waste time before their work is accepted. However, if the authors choose journals that are of much lower quality than the work submitted, then they miss the chance of having this work published in more reputable journals. Naturally, proving/disproving this hypothesis will be influenced by the assumption that papers may only be submitted once. We believe resubmitting usually requires the creation of news versions, which we postpone for future (and more advanced) simulations. Nevertheless, the current simulation may illustrate the effort, time, and potential gain in reputation that could be wasted by preferring one submission strategy over another.

The third hypothesis implies that it would be more profitable, in terms of reputation, to spend more time on producing few high quality research papers than numerous papers of lower quality. This, we believe, lowers the dissemination overhead in researchers' contributions and encourages researchers to spend more time on high quality research, as opposed to wasting time on repackaging already existing ideas for the sole purpose of increasing reputation.

The following section presents the results of the simulations that were run to test the above three hypotheses.

6   Results and Analysis

For our simulation, we choose to simulate a research community composed of a fixed set of 3 journals and 45 researchers. The 3 journals represent a top journal, a mediocre one, and a poor one. The 45 researchers are divided into three main categories (15 authors per category) that represent top quality researchers, mediocre ones, and poor ones. The simulation then runs for 10 time-steps, where each time-step represents one calendar year. In other words, our simulated example represents a fixed community of 45 researchers with varying behaviour and its evolution over 10 years.

At each time-step, papers are added following the constraints of the various profiles. With the addition of each paper, the following measures are calculated: first, the OpinioNet reputation of the papers affected by this addition, and second, the OpinioNet reputation of authors affected by this addition. The evolution of these measures along time is then plotted for further analysis.

Evaluating Hypothesis 1. Recall that researchers are already divided into 3 groups: top quality researchers, mediocre ones, and poor ones. In this experiment, we divide the researchers of each group into 3 sub-groups: those that collaborate with top quality authors, those that collaborate with mediocre authors, and those that collaborate with low quality authors. All the other values defining the researchers' profiles are kept fixed on average values. For example, all researchers' submission strategies are 'risk-neutral'.

The results are presented by Figs. 1, 2, and 3. Note that solid lines represent the reputation of the authors that collaborate with top quality authors, dashed lines represent the reputation of the authors that collaborate with mediocre authors, and dotted lines represent the reputation of authors that collaborate with low quality authors. The range of a reputation measure, as enforced by OpinioNet, is $[0, 1]$, where 0 represents the worst reputation possible and 1 represents the best. Hence, a change in reputation that may visually seem rather slight, could be substantively significant. Also note that since there are 5 authors in each sub-category, the represented values are the mean obtained for all authors in a given category. For this reason, we believe there is no need to repeat each simulation more than once, since we are already analysing the mean of 5 authors.

Figure 1 illustrates that top quality researchers are not very susceptible to the quality of their coauthors. On the other hand, Fig. 2 illustrates that mediocre researchers can do much better if they collaborate with top quality researchers. And the most susceptible of all are poor quality researchers who can do better by collaborating with mediocre researchers, and much better by collaborating with top quality researchers, as illustrated by Fig. 3.

Naturally, these results are the effect of our assumption that the quality of a research work is equal to or greater than the quality of the best author. However, even with a much more lenient assumption that computes the quality of a paper to be the mean of the quality of its authors, we still obtain similar results (which we do not present in this paper due to space limitations), although with much milder curves, compared to those of Figs. 2 and 3.

In summary, our results confirm Hypothesis 1, which states that *the better the quality of the researcher, the less susceptible they are to the quality of their coauthors.*

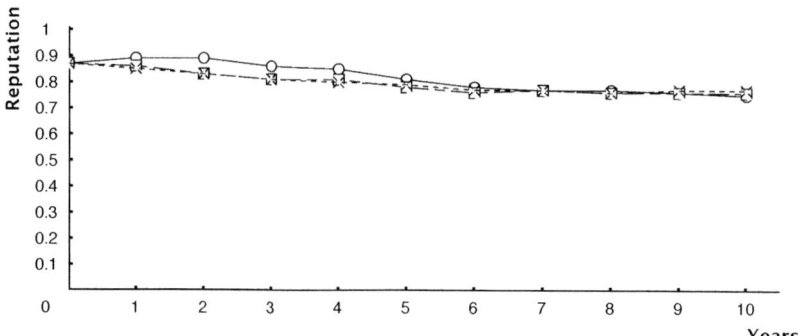

Fig. 1. Reputation of top quality authors w.r.t. the quality of their coauthors

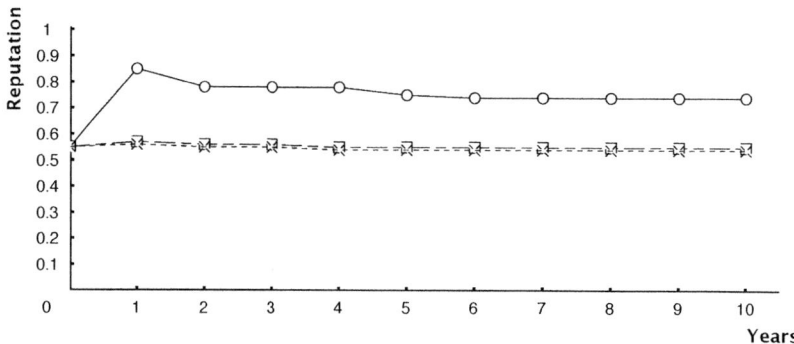

Fig. 2. Reputation of mediocre quality authors w.r.t. the quality of their coauthors

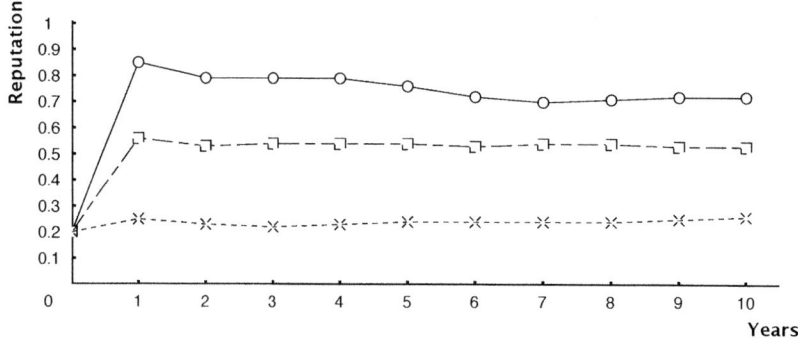

Fig. 3. Reputation of poor quality authors w.r.t. the quality of their coauthors

Evaluating Hypothesis 2. In this experiment, we divide the researchers of each group (i.e. the top quality researchers, the mediocre ones, and the low quality ones) into 3 sub-groups: those with a 'risk-seeking' submission strategy, those with a 'risk-neutral' submission strategy, and those with a 'risk-averse' submission strategy. All the other values defining their profiles are kept fixed on average values.

The results of this experiment are presented by Fig. 4, where solid lines represent the reputation of the authors with a 'risk-seeking' submission strategy, dashed lines represent the reputation of the authors with a 'risk-neutral' submission strategy, and dotted lines represent the reputation of authors with a 'risk-averse' submission strategy. Again, the represented values are the mean obtained for all authors in a given category.

Figure 4 refutes Hypothesis 2, which states that *it is more profitable to follow a risk-neutral submission strategy*, by showing that it is only the top researchers that are susceptible to changes in the submission strategy, and the 'risk-neutral' strategy need not be the ideal one. It seems that the submission strategy does not have a major impact on low quality and mediocre researchers. However, top researchers should continue to give their best (i.e. by submitting to top quality journals regularly); otherwise, their reputation would decrease with lower quality journals (as well as with the decay of information, as enforced by the OpinioNet reputation model which assumes that the value of any piece of information decreases with time [3]).

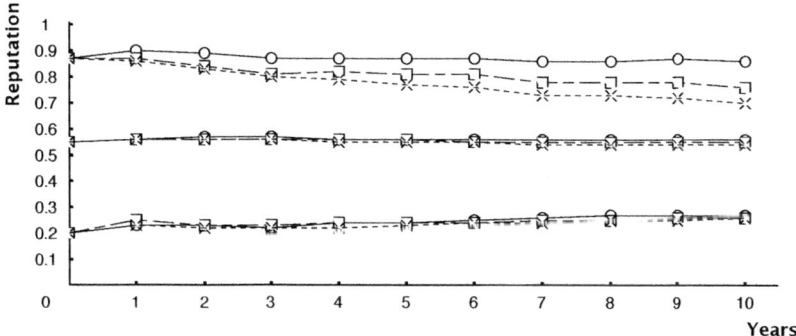

Fig. 4. Reputation of authors w.r.t. their submission strategies

To understand this simulation better, we repeat the same experiment, modifying the intrinsic quality of the researcher to evolve by adopting the researcher's reputation. This assumes that researchers intrinsic quality can get better or worse with time, depending on where they publish. Of course, this is a strong assumption, but it is a simplification which is good enough to represent that a researcher can get better by climbing the ladder one step at a time.[6] The results are presented in Fig. 5, which illustrates that low quality researchers can now

---

[6] We note that the impact of this modification (which considers evolving researchers) was mild with respect to the other simulations. Hence, these results were omitted due to space limitations.

learn from their experiences, and when they get their papers accepted in higher quality journals, their intrinsic quality increases, making it possible for them to climb the ladder one step at a time.

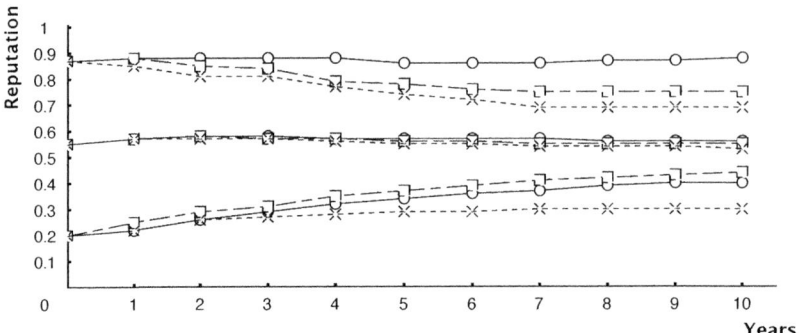

Fig. 5. Reputation of evolving authors w.r.t. their submission strategies

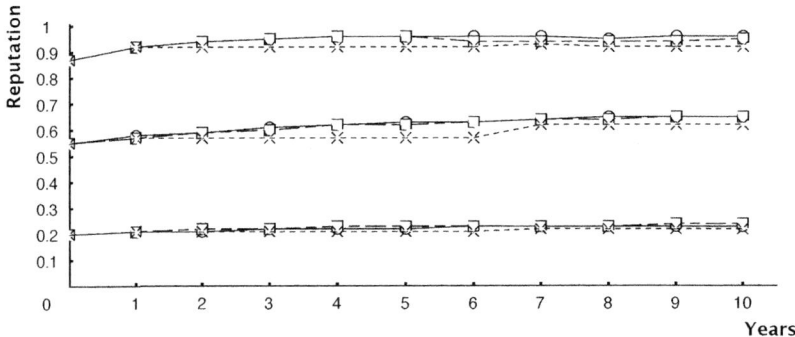

Fig. 6. Reputation of authors w.r.t. their productivity level

Evaluating Hypothesis 3. In this experiment, we divide the researchers of each group (i.e. the top quality researchers, the mediocre ones, and the low quality ones) into 3 sub-groups: those with a high productivity level, those with a medium productivity level, and those with low quality research and a high productivity level. We note that the productivity level represents the number of papers produced per year.[7] Again, all the other values defining the researchers' profiles are kept fixed on average values.

---

[7] Of course, the notion of productivity should not be restricted to the number of papers written per year. However, since the proposed simulation focuses on the publication process, and since other productivity measures cannot be easily detected, we choose to represent the productivity level as the number of papers written per year.

The results of this experiment are presented by Fig. 6, where solid lines represent the reputation of authors with a high productivity level, dashed lines represent the reputation of authors with a mediocre productivity level, and dotted lines represent the reputation of authors with a low productivity level. Again, the represented values are the mean obtained for all authors in a given category.

The results show that those who focus on the quantity cannot do any better than those who focus on the quality of their work, confirming hypothesis 3, which states that *it is more profitable to produce few high quality papers than several low quality ones.*

7   Conclusion

This paper has presented a simulator that simulates the details of the publication process, from writing papers and submitting them to journals, to the review process and the final decision of accepting/rejecting papers. The simulator is rich enough to be used in analysing different aspects of the publication process. However, this paper has focused on using it to verify the OpinioNet reputation model's success in encouraging 'good' behaviour, such as encouraging the focus on the quality of work produced as opposed to its quantity.

Further analysis could still be done on hypotheses 1–3. We also plan to extend our future simulations for testing additional hypotheses such as: *Is it more profitable to repackage one's research work into different versions?* Additionally, future work may also consider (and simulate) citations as another source of opinions, take into consideration the evolution of papers by introducing new versions, and so on.

Acknowledgements. This work has been supported by the LiquidPublications project (funded by the European Commission's FET programme) and the Agreement Technologies project (funded by CONSOLIDER CSD 2007-0022, INGENIO 2010).

References

1. Casati, F., Giunchiglia, F., Marchese, M.: Publish and perish: why the current publication and review model is killing research and wasting your money. Ubiquity 2007, 3:1–3:1 (January 2007), http://doi.acm.org/10.1145/1226694.1226695
2. Osman, N., Sabater-Mir, J., Sierra, C., de Pinninck Bas, A.P., Imran, M., Marchese, M., Ragone, A.: Credit attribution for liquid publications. Deliverable D4.1, LiquidPublications Project (June 2010)
3. Osman, N., Sierra, C., Sabater-Mir, J.: Propagation of opinions in structural graphs. In: Coelho, H., Studer, R., Wooldridge, M. (eds.) Proceeding of the 19th European Conference on Artificial Intelligence (ECAI 2010). Frontiers in Artificial Intelligence and Applications, vol. 215, pp. 595–600. IOS Press, Amsterdam (2010), http://dx.doi.org/10.3233/978-1-60750-606-5-595

4. Osman, N., Sierra, C., Sabater-Mir, J., Wakeling, J.R., Simon, J., Origgi, G., Casati, R.: LiquidPublications and its technical and legal challenges. In: Bourcier, D., Casanovas, P., de Rosnay, M.D., Maracke, C. (eds.) Intelligent Multimedia: Managing Creative Works in a Digital World, vol. 8, pp. 321–336. European Press Academic Publishing, Florence (2010)
5. Peleg, S., Werman, M., Rom, H.: A unified approach to the change of resolution: Space and gray-level. IEEE Transactions on Pattern Analysis and Machine Intelligence 11(7), 739–742 (1989)
6. Pinyol, I., Sabater-Mir, J., Cuní, G.: How to talk about reputation using a common ontology: From definition to implementation. In: Proceedings of the Ninth Workshop on Trust in Agent Societies, Hawaii, USA, pp. 90–101 (2007)

Agent-Based Modeling of the Prediction Markets for Political Elections

Tongkui Yu[1,2] and Shu-Heng Chen[1,*]

[1] AI-ECON Research Center, Department of Economics,
National Chengchi University, Taipei 11605
chen.shuheng@gmail.com
[2] School of Computer and Information Science, Southwest University,
Chongqing 400715

Abstract. We propose a simple agent-based model of the political election prediction market which reflects the intrinsic feature of the prediction market as an information aggregation mechanism. Each agent has a vote, and all agents' votes determine the election result. Some of the agents participate in the prediction market. Agents form their beliefs by observing their neighbors' voting disposition, and trade with these beliefs by following some forms of the zero-intelligence strategy. In this model, the mean price of the market is used as a forecast of the election result. We study the effect of the radius of agents' neighborhood and the geographical distribution of information on the prediction accuracy. In addition, we also identify one of the mechanisms which can replicate the favorite-longshot bias, a stylized fact in the prediction market. This model can then provide a framework for further analysis on the prediction market when market participants have more sophisticated trading behavior.

Keywords: Prediction market, Agent based simulation, Information aggregation mechanism, Prediction accuracy, Zero-intelligence agents, Favorite-longshot bias.

1 Introduction

Prediction Markets, sometimes referred to as "information markets", "idea futures" or "event futures", are markets where participants trade contracts whose payoffs are tied to a future event, thereby yielding prices that can be interpreted as market-aggregated forecasts [1]. To predict whether a particular event (say, some candidate winning the election) will happen, a common approach is to create a security that will pay out some predetermined amount (say, 1 dollar) if the event happens, and let agents trade this security until a stable price emerges; the price can then be interpreted as the consensus probability that the event will happen. There is mounting evidence that such markets can help to produce forecasts of event outcomes with a lower prediction error than conventional forecasting methods [2].

---

* Corresponding author.

D. Villatoro, J. Sabater-Mir, and J.S. Sichman (Eds.): MABS 2011, LNAI 7124, pp. 31–43, 2012.

To explain the efficiency of the prediction market in relation to aggregate information, many researchers use the efficient market hypothesis which attributes the market efficiency to a pool of knowledgeable traders who are capable of setting prices and acting without bias [3]. While Manski proposed a model [4] to find that price is a particular quantile of the distribution of traders' beliefs, price does not reveal the mean belief that traders hold, but does yield a bound on the mean belief. It can explain both the market efficiency and another stylized fact in prediction markets - *favorite-longshot bias* - which means that likely events (favorite) are underpriced or underestimated and unlikely events (longshot) are overpriced or overestimated [5]. Wolfers and Zitzewitz provided sufficient conditions under which prediction market prices coincide with average beliefs among traders in a model with log-utility agents [6]. Snowberg and Wolfers found evidence that misperceptions of probability drive the favorite-long shot bias, as suggested by prospect theory [7].

In this paper, we follow the recent research trend in agent-based prediction markets, and construct a spatial agent-based political futures markets based on the two-dimensional cellular automata. We begin this study with the device of zero-intelligence agents which was introduced into agent-based economic modeling by Gode and Sunder [8] and later on was applied to prediction markets by Othman [9]. However, instead of studying the general-purpose prediction markets, we focus on the political futures market, which, needless to say, is one of the most active application areas of prediction markets. This focus motivates us a spatial extension of the Othman's model. This extension also enables us to address a number of issues which cannot not be easily approached by either the neoclassical models of prediction markets [4,7] or by agent-based prediction markets without spatial configurations. Specifically, the question is how exactly the information dissemination affect the information aggregation given that agents can only form their beliefs based on their information from their surroundings. Second, to take into account the geographical or social segregation phenomena, as analyzed by Schelling[10], we also study how clusters and their size may affect the operation efficiency of the political future markets. Using this Schelling-lik model, we can study the effect of cluster size to the prediction accuracy of the political future markets.

The rest of the paper is organized as follows. Section 2 introduces our spatial agent-based model of prediction markets, built on the very simple behavioral assumption of agents, namely, the zero-intelligent agents. Section 3 presents the agent-based simulation results. Section 3.1 shows that, by very simple behavioral assumptions of the traders, our agent-based model can replicate the well-known favorite-longshot bias. Section 3.2 further shows the prediction accuracy in monotonically (linearly) increasing in terms of the neighborhood size. Section 3.3 studies the effect of the geographical distribution of information on prediction accuracy. We find that, given the neighborhood size, there is a non-linear relation between block size and prediction error. Section 3.4 searches for the possible origins of the favorite-longshot bias, and indicates how the bid and ask behavior can attribute to the emergence of this bias. Concluding remarks are given in Section 4.

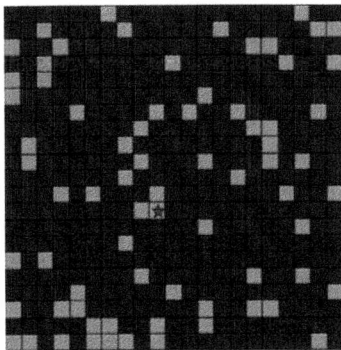

Fig. 1. Illustration of voter's political preference in a two-dimensional grid

2 Basic Model

In a society represented by a two-dimensional torus grid, each element is a person, and each person has his own disposition on the vote for some candidate, blue for supporting (1) and green for not supporting (0) as in Figure 1. Figure 1 is simply for the illustrative purpose. In our simulation, we consider a more extensive model with a grid size of 200×200. Furthermore, in the simulations, the agents' voting disposition is randomly initialized with a given overall support ratio. This parameter is denoted as *SupportRatio*.

Some agents randomly sampled from the entire population will participate in a prediction market which provides a winner-take-all contract that pays a dollar if the candidate wins, and pays nothing if the candidate loses.[1] Each agent has a belief (subjective probability) $b_i \in [0, 1]$ that a candidate will win. This subjective belief is formed based on the sample statistics (sample mean) of the voting disposition of agent's neighbors. His/her neighbors consist of the center node (the agent himself) and the nearest Moore neighbors. Hence, the neighborhood has 9 agents for neighborhood radius $r = 1$, and 25 agents for neighborhood radius $r = 2$, as in Figure 2. For the agent marked with the red star, his own vote disposition is to support the candidate, and there are two other agents in his neighborhood with radius $r = 1$ who also support the candidate (Figure 2, left panel), so his belief is $b_i = 3/9 = 1/3$. If the radius $r = 2$ (Figure 2, right panel), his belief is $b_i = 5/25 = 1/5$.

This belief (subjective probability) will be taken as the reference price in the following sense that the agent would like to sell the future with any price higher than this one, and would like buy with any price lower than this one. More specifically, by using the device of the *zero-intelligence agent*, the agent

---

[1] The winner-take-all market and the share market are the two commonly used designs for the prediction markets. For the latter, the market participant is paid, according to the election results, by the final voting share of the candidate. Our agent-based model introduced here is equally applicable to the share market.

(a) r=1   (b) r=2

Fig. 2. Moore neighborhood of the agent in a two-dimensional grid

with belief b_i places a bid order for one share of the event at a price *uniformly* on $[0, b_i]$, or an ask order for one share at a price *uniformly* on $[b_i, 1]$, as in figure 3. The role of the agent, a buyer (to bid) or a seller (to ask), is randomly determined with equal probability. In vein of the zero-intelligence design, the learning or strategic behavior of agents is not taken into account. Agents do not "observe" (care) current market prices, and do not react to the result of their previous actions; they keep no record of previous unfinished orders.

This is a device of the *zero-intelligence agent* initiated by Gode and Sunder [8], which is now widely used in the agent-based models. The zero-intelligence agent is a randomly-behaving agent or, more precisely speaking, an entropy-maximizing agent. Since normal traders would not propose or accept a deal which would obviously lead to economic loss or not lead to welfare improvement, under no further information on what else they will do, the design of the zero-intelligence agent is *minimally prejudiced* in the sense of entropy maximization. The *uniform distribution* is employed here to realize the maximum entropy. Othman also carried out this design in his pioneering study on the agent-based prediction market [9].

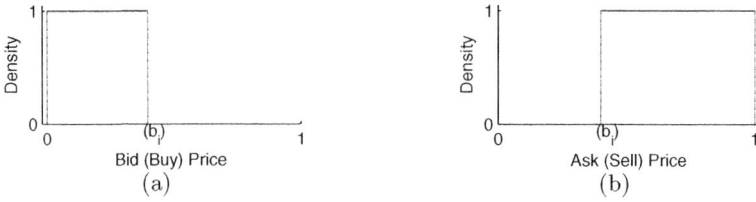

Fig. 3. Order price formation

Following [9], the transactions are closed by the mechanism of continuous double exchange. Agents place buy or sell orders continuously. Once the highest-priced bid exceeds the lowest-priced ask, a trade occurs at the price of the order which was placed first. The paper, however, differs from [9] by explicitly embedding the agent-based prediction market within the network structure, a checkerboard as demonstrated in Figure 1. We consider this as a first attempt to

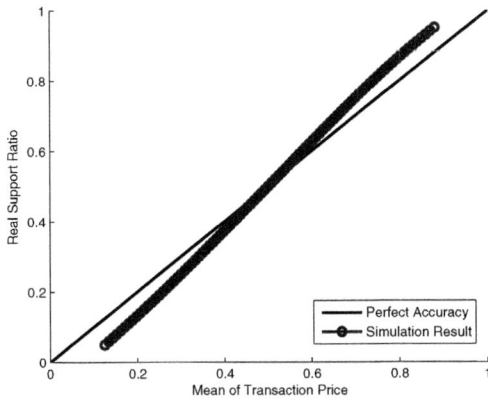

Fig. 4. Typical simulation result and favorite-longshot bias

hybridize the spatial agent-based political election models and the agent-based prediction markets for political elections.

The procedure of the model is described by the pseudocode in Algorithm 1.

3   Simulation and Analysis

We perform a great deal of simulations and try to find the regularity in the simulated data.

3.1   Prediction Power and Favorite-Longshot Bias

In the agent-based model of the political election prediction market, the mean of the transaction price is normally taken as a good predictor of the real support ratio in the overall population. Figure 4 provides the relationship between the real support ratio (vertical axis) and the mean of the transaction price (horizontal axis) in typical simulations with the neighborhood radius $r = 1$. This simulation is conducted in a 200 by 200 checkerboard with 40,000 agents ($N = 40,000$), one in each cell (a checkerboard with full size). For each given support ratio, the continuous double auction is run once for 40,000 rounds. We then try support ratios from 0.1 to 0.9 with an increment of 0.01; in other words, a total of 81 support ratios are tried. We then plot the mean of the transaction price over the 40,000 rounds for each support ratio in Figure 4. As we can see from that figure, the mean transaction price can trace the true support ratio to some degree.

At the same time, the simulation replicates the favorite-longshot bias, a stylized fact in the prediction market. We can find that unlikely events (bottom-left in Figure 4) are overpriced, and likely events (top-right in Figure 4) are underpriced.

Algorithm 1. Simulation Procedure

Require: Total number of agents N; Rounds of the market M; The overall support
ratio $SupportRatio$;
Ensure: Transaction price history $TransactionPrice$
// INITIALIZATION
Generate a random number $rndNum$ uniformly from 0 to 1
for each agent in the population **do**
  if $rndNum < SupportRatio$ **then**
    Set his voting disposition as supporting (1)
  else
    Set his voting disposition as not supporting (0)
  end if
end for
// RUNNING THE MARKET
for round $\in [1, M]$ **do**
  Choose an agent randomly from the whole population
  Get the voting dispositions of his neighbors
  Set the agent's belief b as the number of supporters over neighborhood size
  Generate a random number $rndNum$ uniformly from 0 to 1
  if $rndNum < 0.5$ **then**
    Set the order side to 1 (buy)
    Set the $OrderPrice$ as a random number uniformly drawn from 0 to b
    Get the $MinSellPrice$ in the $SellOrderList$
    if $OrderPrice > MinSellPrice$ **then**
      Insert a transaction in the $TransactionList$ with $MinSellPrice$
    else
      Insert a buy order with $OrderPrice$ in the $BuyOrderList$
    end if
  else
    Set the order side to 0 (sell)
    Set the $OrderPrice$ as a random number uniformly drawn from b to 1
    Get the $MaxBuyPrice$ in the $BuyOrderList$
    if $OrderPrice < MaxBuyPrice$ **then**
      Insert a transaction in the $TransactionList$ with $MaxBuyPrice$
    else
      Insert a sell order with $OrderPrice$ in the $SellOrderList$
    end if
  end if
end for

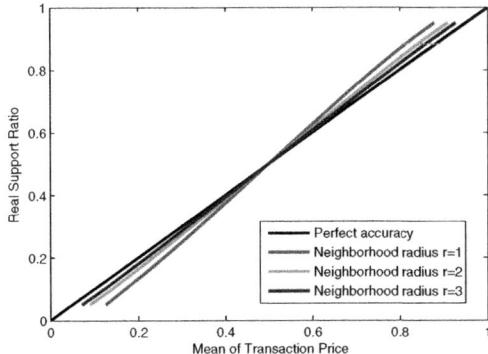

Fig. 5. Neighborhood radius and prediction accuracy

3.2   Neighborhood Scope and Prediction Accuracy

We investigate the effect of the neighborhood scope on the prediction accuracy. Figure 5 provides the relationship between the real support ratio (vertical axis) and the mean of the transaction price (horizontal axis) in typical simulations with different neighborhood radii $r = 1, 2$ and 3. We can find that the prediction accuracy of the prediction market increases as the neighborhood scope increases. It is easy to understand that the more information that each participant has, the more accurate the prediction that the market can provide. This result is similar to the work of Othman [9]. However, we obtain the result with a totally different basic assumption. We use rather simple assumption that the agent forms his belief by observing his neighbors' voting deposition, while Othman's work requires specific distribution of belief. With this distinction, we attribute the extent of the bias to the amount of individual information that each individual agent has, while Othman's work attributes it to the arbitrarily specified belief distribution.

To measure the prediction accuracy of a prediction market, we define a variable referred to as the mean squared error

$$\rho = \frac{\sum_1^S (MeanPrice_i - SupportRatio_i)^2}{S}, \tag{1}$$

where $i = 1 : S$ is the number of simulations. A larger mean squared error implies less accurate prediction, while a smaller one implies more accurate prediction, and $\rho = 0$ implies perfect accuracy. With the same neighborhood radius, we simulate $S(S = 200)$ times with $SupportRatio$ linearly spaced between 0 and 1 and calculate the prediction accuracy. Figure 6 presents the effect of the neighborhood radius r (horizontal) on the prediction accuracy (vertical axis). The larger the neighborhood radius r, the more information agents have, and the more accurate prediction the market can provide.

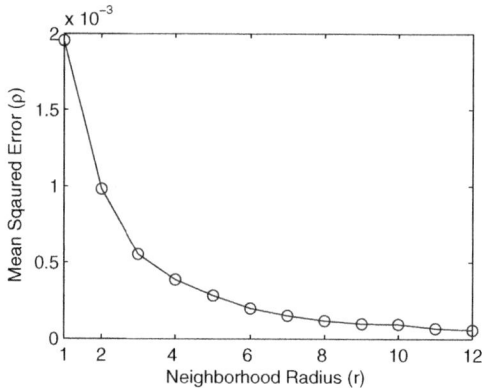

Fig. 6. Effect of neighborhood radius on the prediction accuracy

3.3 Information Distribution and Prediction Accuracy

In a real political election, the voting deposition may be clustered. Some places may be dominated by the supporter of one candidate, and most of the population may support the other candidate elsewhere. So the information is not well scattered. We wish to study the effect of information distribution on the prediction accuracy. To this end, we manipulate the block size of voting disposition to represent different information distributions.

When initializing the voting disposition of the agents, we use different granularities or block size s. If the block size $s = 1$, we initialize the agents' voting disposition one by one; if the block size $s=2$, we initialize the agents' voting disposition two by two, i.e., all four agents in the 2×2 sub-grid have the same voting disposition randomly generated according to the specified support ratio. Figure 7 illustrates a comparison of information distributions with block sizes $s = 1$ and 2 under the same support ratio 0.3.

Figure 8 depicts the effect of voting disposition block size on prediction accuracy with neighborhood radii $r = 2, 3, 5$ and 7. We can find the nonlinear relationship between the block size and mean squared error. The mean squared error is the largest when the voting disposition block size is close to the neighborhood radius, and the market prediction power is the least accurate. The farther away the voting disposition block size is from the neighborhood radius, the smaller is the mean squared error, the more accurate is the market prediction. This result is confirmed by figure 9 which provides the combination effect of block size and neighborhood radius to the mean squared error. Further research is needed to understand this phenomenon.

3.4 The Origin of the Favorite-Longshot Bias

So far, we have shown that we can replicate the favorite-longshot bias. The advantage of using agent-based models is that we can go further to ask whether we

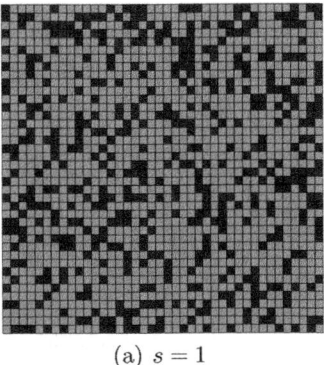 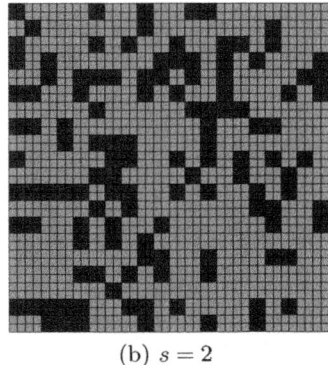

(a) $s = 1$ (b) $s = 2$

Fig. 7. Comparison of information distributions with different block sizes of voting disposition

can trace the possible source of this bias. To find the mechanism that produces the favorite-longshot bias, we have performed some experiments. One possible origin of the favorite-longshot bias is the *price formation mechanism*; the baseline version closes transactions at the price of the order (bid or ask) which was first placed. An alternative price formation mechanism is to take average of the bid and ask, instead of only one of the two (the earlier posted one). Nonetheless, our simulation shows that the favorite-longshot bias still exists with this modification.

The other possible origin of the favorite-longshot bias is the *order-formation mechanism*. The baseline version is that an agent can submit a bid between zero and his belief b_i or an ask at a price between b_i and 1 (as in Figure 3). When the agents' belief is not equal to 0.5, there is an inherent asymmetry between the range of bid and the range of ask. This may lead to the favorite-longshot bias.

We test the hypothesis by proposing a symmetric order price formation mechanism where an agent submit a bid at a price drawn randomly from $[b_i - \delta, b_i]$, or submit an ask at a price drawn randomly from $[b_i, b_i + \delta]$ as in Figure 10(a) . We find that the favorite-longshot bias disappears in this specification as in 10(b). Moreover, we perform a simulation using the designed asymmetric order price formation mechanism, where the prices of buy orders are uniformly on $[b_i - \delta, b_i]$ and the prices of sell orders are uniformly on $[b_i, b_i + 2\delta]$ as in Figure 10(c), and we find that the prices are all overvalued as in figure 10(d). Furthermore, if the prices of buy orders are uniformly on $[b_i - 2\delta, b_i]$ and the prices of sell orders are uniformly on $[b_i, b_i + \delta]$ as in Figure 10(e), the prices are all undervalued as in Figure 10(f). So we can come to the conclusion that the asymmetry of the order-price mechanism is the one of possible origins of the favorite-longshot bias.

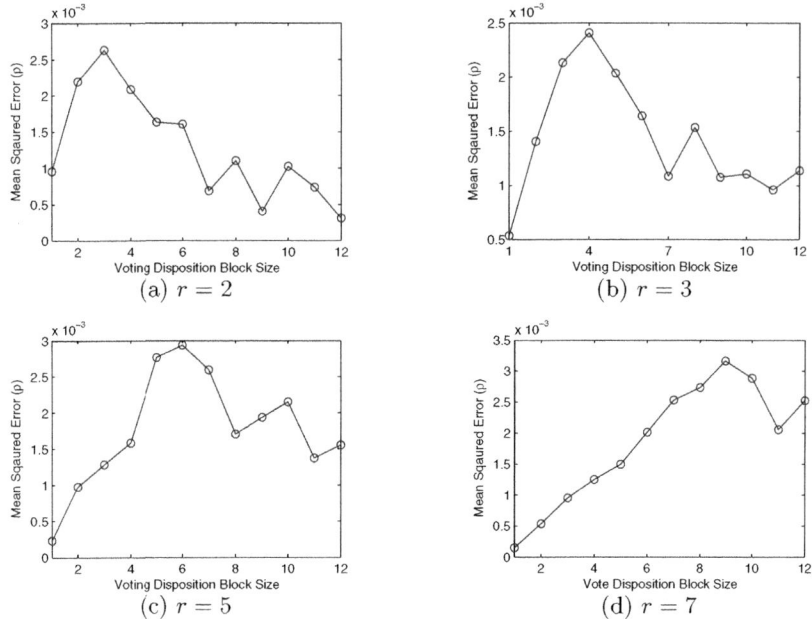

Fig. 8. The effect of voting disposition block size on prediction accuracy

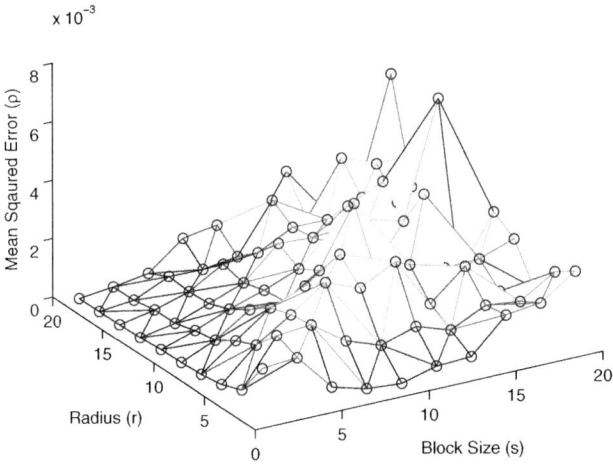

Fig. 9. Block Size, neighborhood radius and prediction accuracy

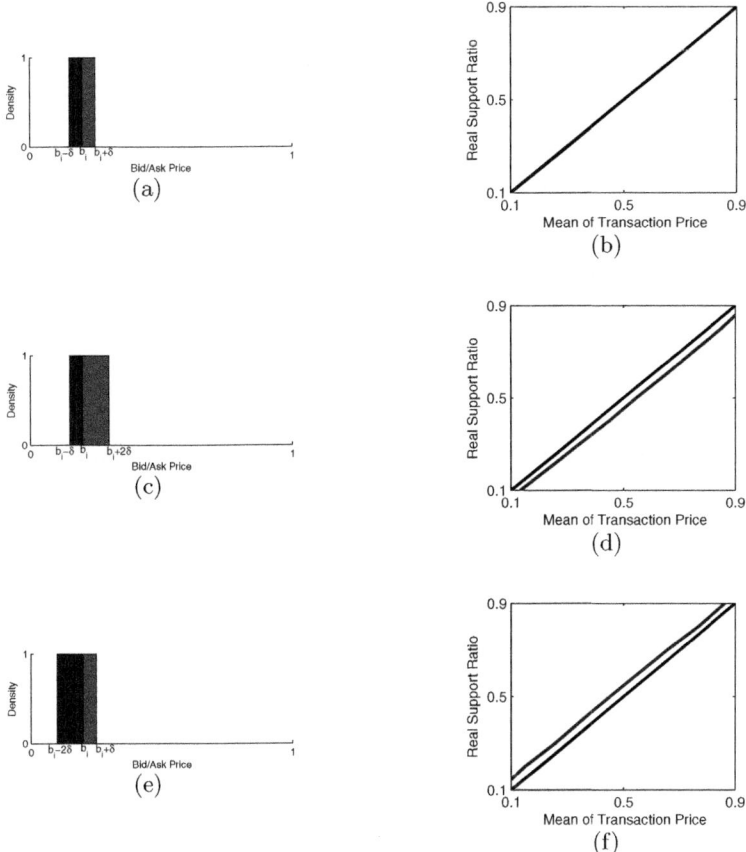

Fig. 10. Order price formation mechanism and favorite-longshot bias

4   Conclusion

Prediction markets and experimental markets are, so far, the two real tests for the Hayek hypothesis on the market mechanism as functions of information aggregation and information externality. Given the competitiveness and the popularity of the ideas of prediction markets, it would be imperative to see how this idea actually works, and agent-based modeling can provide possible rich settings to examine their functions. In this specific paper, we show how the well-known favorite-longshot bias can be replicated through one version of our agent-based model; but we also show how different settings may cause this bias to disappear. Neighborhood size and cluster size all have their effects on the accuracy of the prediction markets, but the cross interaction of the two needs to be further examined.

One extension of this paper is to replace the zero-intelligence agents with agents behaving more realistically. This is the part which behavior finance may shed light on. As what has been analyzed in this paper, the favorite-longshot bias can be caused by the asymmetric trading behavior of the agent, and the bias disappears when symmetric trading behavior is imposed. However, regardless of being symmetric or asymmetric, the zero-intelligence trading behavior characterized by the uniform-distributional bids or asks is not realistic, at least for economists.[2] Therefore, one could argue that the favorite-longshot bias can equally likely be caused by more deliberate and sophisticate trading behavior. If so, what would be the minimal description of the "smart" behavior leading to this bias is a question for the future of the research. Finally, whether the simulation results can have important implications for the design of the prediction market is also an issue for further study [11].

Acknowledgements. An earlier version of the paper was presented at the *12th International Workshop on Multi-Agent-Based Simulation* (**MABS 2011**), Taipei, May 2, 2011. The authors are grateful to the three anonymous referees and Prof Van Dyke Parumak for their suggestions made to the paper. The financial support from the Chung-Hwa Development Foundation, the NSC Grant 98-2410-H-004-045-MY3 and the Southwest University Science Grant SWUQ2006022 is also gratefully acknowledged.

References

1. Wolfers, J., Zitzewitz, E.: Prediction Markets. J. Econ. Perspect. 18(2), 107–126 (2004)
2. Arrow, K.J., Forsythe, R., Gorham, M., et al.: The Promise of Prediction Markets. Science 320, 877–878 (2008)
3. Forsythe, R., Nelson, F., Neumann, G., Wright, J.: Anatomy of an Experimental Political Stock Market. Am. Econ. Rev. 82(5), 1142–1161 (1992)
4. Manski, C.F.: Interpreting the Predictions of Prediction Markets. Econ. Lett. 91(3), 425–429 (2006)
5. Wolfers, J., Zitzewitz, E.: Five Open Questions About Prediction Markets. In: Hahn, R.W. (ed.) Information Markets: A New Way of Making Decisions. AEI Press (2008)
6. Wolfers, J., Zitzewitz, E.: Interpreting Prediction Market Prices as Probabilities. NBER Working Paper No. 10359 (2005)
7. Snowberg, E., Wolfers, J.: Explaining the Favorite-Longshot Bias: Is it Risk-Love or Misperceptions? J. Polit. Econ. 118(4), 723–746 (2010)
8. Gode, D., Sunder, S.: Allocative Efficiency of Markets with Zero-Intelligence Traders: Market as a Partial Substitute for Individual Rationality. J. of Polit. Econ. 101(1), 119–137 (1993)

---

[2] For example, as one of the referees has correctly pointed out that our zero-intelligence design means that an agent that believes the share is worth 0.5 is equally likely not to sell it for 0.6 or 0.9.

9. Othman, A.: Zero-intelligence Agents in Prediction Markets. In: Proceedings of AAMAS 2008, pp. 879–886 (2008)
10. Schelling, T.: Dynamic models of segregation. Journal of Mathematical Sociology 1, 143–186 (1971)
11. Chen, S.-H., Tung, C.-Y., Tai, C.-C., Chie, B.-T., Chou, T.-C., Wang, S.: Prediction Markets: A Study on the Taiwan Experience. In: Williams, L. (ed.) Prediction Markets: Theory and Applications, ch. 11, pp. 137–156. Routledge, London (2011)

Using Multi-agent Simulation
to Improve the Security of Maritime Transit

Ondřej Vaněk, Michal Jakob, Ondřej Hrstka, and Michal Pěchouček

Agent Technology Center, Dept. of Cybernetics,
Faculty of Electrical Engineering, Czech Technical University,
Technická 2, Praha 6, Czech Republic
{vanek,jakob,hrstka,pechoucek}@agents.fel.cvut.cz
http://agents.fel.cvut.cz

Abstract. Despite their use for modeling traffic in ports and regional waters, multi-agent simulations have not yet been applied to model maritime traffic on a global scale. We therefore propose a fully agent-based, data-driven model of global maritime traffic, focusing primarily on modeling transit through piracy-affected waters. The model employs finite state machines to represent the behavior of several classes of vessels and can accurately replicate global shipping patterns and approximate real-world distribution of pirate attacks. We apply the model to the problem of optimizing the Gulf of Aden group transit. The results demonstrate the usefulness of agent-based modeling for evaluating and improving operational counter-piracy policies and measures.

Due to its inherent dynamism, distribution and complexity of dependencies, traffic and transportation is a domain particularly suitable for the application of multi-agent techniques. This has been reflected in the number of multi-agent simulations developed in the field of air traffic (e.g. [18]) and ground transportation [2,14]. The key motivation behind these models is to better understand the behavior of transportation systems and to evaluate novel mechanisms for improving it.

In the maritime domain, existing models focus on traffic in ports and regional, near shore waters [3,15,10]. High-level equation-based models are typically used, which have difficulties capturing vessel interactions and more complex dynamics of maritime traffic. In contrast, our proposed model focuses on modeling global maritime traffic and employs a fully agent-based, microsimulation approach. Such a model is pivotal in the development of measures for countering the complex problem of maritime piracy, which presents a growing threat to global shipping industry and consequently international trade. In 2010 alone, 53 merchant vessels were hijacked and 1181 crew members held hostage [11] and the numbers continued to rise in the first half of 2011.

The proposed simulation model is the first agent-based model focusing on maritime traffic and piracy. It models the operation of all key actors in piracy scenarios, i.e., the long-range merchant vessels, pirate vessels and navy patrols. Although the simulation is geared towards maritime piracy, it is rather general

D. Villatoro, J. Sabater-Mir, and J.S. Sichman (Eds.): MABS 2011, LNAI 7124, pp. 44–58, 2012.

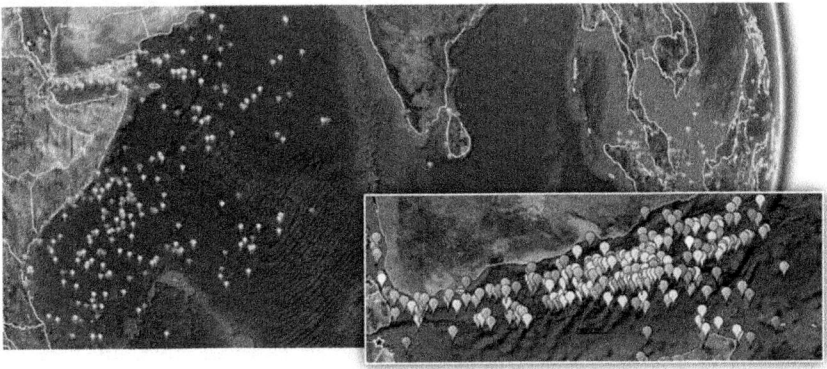

Fig. 1. Locations of pirate incidents over the last 5 years

and applicable to other problems in maritime transportation. As an illustrative application, we apply the simulation to optimize the group transit scheme established to improve the security of transit through the notorious Gulf of Aden.

Section 1 provides a brief introduction to the domain and reviews current anti-piracy measures. Sections 2.1, 2.2 and 2.3 describe agent-based models of three main classes of vessels. Section 3 describes implementation aspects of the proposed models and Section 4 discusses model validation. Finally, Section 5 describes the application to group transit scheme optimization.

1   Domain Background

In this section, we briefly describe existing anti-piracy measures and domain facts that are incorporated in the proposed model.

1.1   Piracy Around the Horn of Africa

Over the last years, waters around the Horn of Africa have experienced a steep rise in piracy. For approximately 20 thousand vessels[1] that annually transit the area, insurance rates have increased more than tenfold and the total cost of piracy was estimated at up to US$16 billion in 2008. Although attacks and hijackings used to be concentrated in the Gulf of Aden, in the last two years the pirates have been expanding further from the coast and attacking vessels on the main shipping lanes in the Indian Ocean, more than 1500 nm from the Somali coast (see Figure 1).

1.2   Existing Antipiracy Measures

In order to counter the rising piracy threat, a number of measures have been put into effect in the Horn of Africa area, which encompasses the Gulf of Aden

---

[1] about 40% of the world fleet.

Table 1. IRTC group transit schedule – entry times for vessels travelling at different speeds

Speed	Entry point A – time	Entry point B – time
10 kts	04:00 GMT+3	18:00 GMT+3
12 kts	08:30 GMT+3	00:01 GMT+3
14 kts	11:30 GMT+3	04:00 GMT+3
16 kts	14:00 GMT+3	08:30 GMT+3
18 kts	16:00 GMT+3	10:00 GMT+3

and the West Indian Ocean. Since 2008, transit through the Gulf of Aden itself has been organized – transiting vessels are grouped according to their speed and directed through a narrow transit corridor patrolled by international naval forces.

International Recommended Transit Corridor. Initially introduced in 2008, the *International Recommended Transit Corridor (IRTC)* was amended in 2009 to reflect the revised analysis of piracy in the Gulf of Aden and to incorporate shipping industry feedback. The new corridor has been positioned further from established fishing areas, resulting in a reduction of false piracy alerts[2].

Navy Patrols. Several naval task forces from various countries and allied forces[3] operate in the Gulf of Aden (see [13] for details) to protect the transit corridor and prevent attacks on transiting vessels. Detailed information about the strategy of navy vessels is classified. On a high-level, their coordination is based on a *4W Grid* on which areas of responsibility are assigned [5].

Group Transit Scheme. In August 2010, the *Group Transit Scheme* was introduced to further reduce the risk of pirate attacks on vessels transiting the Gulf of Aden [17]. *Group transits* are designed to group ships into several speed groups in order to leverage additional protection and assurance of traveling in a group. Each transit follows a recommended route through the IRTC at a published speed and schedule, designed to avoid the highest-risk areas and time periods. There is one transit per day for each speed group (see Table 1).

2   Model Description

We employ the agent-based modeling approach – each vessel is implemented as an autonomous agent with its specific behavior, capable of interacting with other

---

[2] MSCHOA, The Maritime Security Centre, Horn of Africa, strongly recommends transiting vessels to follow the corridor to benefit from the protection provided by naval forces.

[3] NATO, Combined Maritime Forces including Japan, China, India, Korea and others.

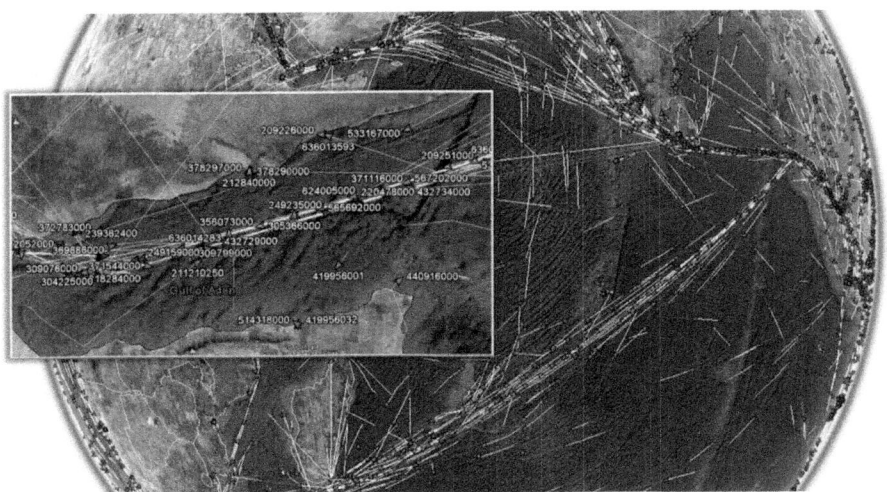

Fig. 2. Merchant vessel traces obtained from satellite AIS data

vessels and the simulated maritime environment. Three categories of vessels are modeled: (1) long-haul merchant vessels, (2) pirate vessels and (3) navy vessels. Each behavior model is based on real-world data. Below, we describe the model for each vessel category.

2.1 Merchant Vessel Model

Merchant vessels, traveling repeatedly between the world's large ports, form the bulk of international maritime traffic. Our agent-based model aims to achieve the same spatio-temporal distribution as the real traffic. We do not simulate physical vessel dynamics and do not yet take into account environmental conditions such as weather or sea currents.

Data Used. Data from the *Automatic Identification System (AIS)* – the most widely used vessel position tracking system – are publicly available[4] and contain time-stamped records of vessel GPS positions along their routes. However, even though it is easy to simply replay the traces, it is not possible to test various hypothetical scenarios (the main reason for the development of the simulation), not to mention low spatial resolution in crucial areas. We thus use AIS data to reconstruct main shipping lanes and traffic density. Furthermore, we use data about geography, including locations of ports, straits, channels or capes through which vessels have to pass while avoiding land, islands and shallow waters.

---

[4] Large databases are available on http://www.vesseltracker.com or http://www.aislive.com.

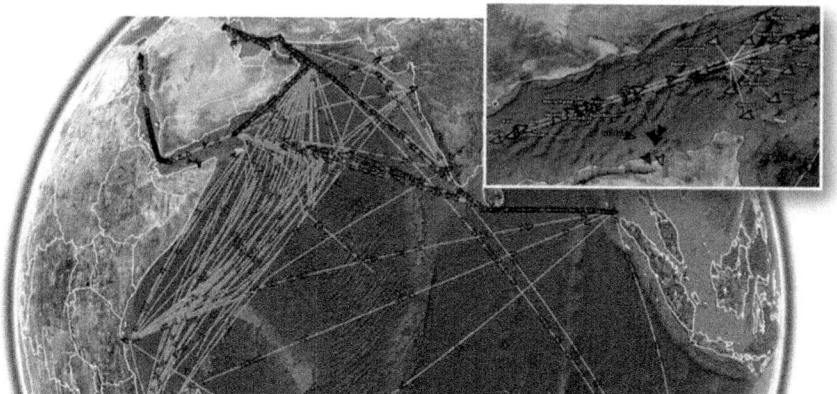

Fig. 3. Simulated traffic – merchant vessels (green) and pirate vessels (red)

AIS Data-based Replicating Traffic Model. In the simplest traffic model, each simulated vessel follows an assigned AIS trace. This way, we are able to re- play real traffic from recorded AIS data (see Figure 2). While easy to implement, this approach has several drawbacks: (1) the AIS data have very low sampling frequencies in crucial areas, such as in the Gulf of Aden; (2) the scalability is limited and the number of agents is limited by the number of available traces; (3) experimentation with alternative shipping routes is not possible; (4) the data may be obsolete and not yet reflect the recent shifts in maritime shipping lanes due to increased pirate activity.

Merchant Vessel Model. To eliminate the above issues, we combined simple AIS replication with route planning algorithms in order to generate realistic merchant vessel traffic. As long as it is safe, vessels follow shortest paths between desired locations, avoiding obstacles. Transit through high-risk areas is handled separately to reflect vessel's tendency to avoid such areas or to use special tactics to make such transit more secure.

To approximate global properties of the real-world merchant vessel traffic, origin-destination matrices are used for trip generation. The simulated vessels plan their routes between ports using the combination of the following planners:

Shortest Path Planning. The shortest route planner is based on the A^* algorithm in a spherical environment with polygonal obstacles. The algorithm employs a pre-calculated visibility graph to speed up search and is guaranteed to find the shortest path [16].

Risk-aware Route Planning. The risk-aware planner is invoked for planning routes through high-risk areas. The planner searches for a route which mini- mizes a weighted sum of route length and the piracy risk along the route. To quantify the risk along a route, we use a spatio-temporal incident density map representing the number of piracy incidents in a given area over a given period of time. By integrating incident density along a vessel route, we obtain the estimate of the number of incidents N that can be expected when following the route. Using the Poisson probability distribution, we then estimate the probability of at least one attack as $1 - e^{-N}$ (for details, see [13]).

Strategic Route Planning. In contrast to the previous two route planners, which reflect practices currently used in the field, the strategic route planning provides an experimental technique for further reducing piracy risk. This game-theoretic route planner explicitly accounts for pirate adaptability and ability to reason about merchant vessel routes and produces routes in an optimally randomized manner, which minimizes the chance of a successful pirate attack (similar to work done by Jain et al. [12]). See [20] for a detailed description of the algorithms.

Group Transit Model. Vessel trajectories are not modified when participating in the group transit scheme and so the generated route does not need to be modified. However, the vessel has to be present at the beginning of the IRTC corridor at a prescribed time (according to the schedule 1) and then continue through the corridor at a prescribed speed. See Section 1.2 for the description of the currently employed group transit schedules and Section 5 for the design of optimal group transit schedules. The implemented group transit model accurately reflects the current state.

2.2 Pirate Vessel Model

Due to the lack of data on real-world pirate vessel movement, an indirect approach is used in modeling pirate behavior.

Data Used. The primary source of information for pirate vessel model are reported descriptions of typical pirate strategies (found e.g. in [8]) which we have translated into executable behavior models (see below). These are then used in conjunction with additional data about real-world pirate activity. Specifically, we use a public dataset [7] of places on the Somali coast known to serve as pirate hubs or ransom anchorages. We also use piracy incident records published since 2005 by the IMB Piracy Reporting Centre[5]. Each record contains the incident location in GPS format, the type of attacked vessel, incident date and the type of attack (see Figure 1 for the visualization of a sample of the dataset). These data are partially used for calibration and partially for validation of the pirate behavior model (see Section 4.2).

Pirate Behavior Model. In order to capture the diversity of real-world pirate strategies (see e.g. [8]) we implemented four different pirate vessel models: (1) *Simple pirate* with a small boat without any means of vessel detection except the direct line of sight (5 nm), (2) *Radar pirate* with a radar extending the

---

[5] http://www.icc-ccs.org/home/piracy-reporting-centre

vessel detection range to 20-50 nm, (3) *AIS pirate* with an AIS interception device monitoring AIS broadcasts and (4) *Mothership pirate* with a medium-size vessel and several boats able to attack vessels up 1500 nm from the Somali coast. The last type can be combined with the radar or AIS interception device to achieve more complex behavior. Additionally, for specific needs of testing game-theoretic routing strategies, we designed an adaptive pirate based on the multi-armed bandit problem [19]. Through trial and error, the adaptive pirate is capable of discovering and exploiting potential vulnerabilities of employed routing and patrolling strategies.

Each pirate agent is initialized in its home port and based on the position of the port, it is assigned its operational zone (Gulf of Aden, Northern or Southern part of Indian Ocean). The pirate operates in cycles, starting and finishing in its home port. Before each cycle, the pirate chooses a position to sail. In the case of the adaptive pirate, this decision is based on the exploration/exploitation algorithm; otherwise the position is chosen randomly from the assigned operational area. Based on the type of vessel used, the pirate has different total amount of time it can spend on the open sea, ranging from a single day in the case of small boats to weeks in the case of motherships.

2.3   Naval Vessel Model

The lack of data and large variation of patrolling strategies – which can vary from active search for pirates to protecting transiting groups of merchant vessels – makes proper modeling of navy vessel agents very difficult. We have thus proposed a minimal model based on the information available. However, as a potential improvement to current practices, we have also proposed a game-theoretic policy for patrolling (see [4] for details).

Data Used. The *4W Grid* [5], dividing the Gulf of Aden into square sectors, is used for coordination of anti-piracy operations. Data about combined task forces CTF-150 and CTF-151 are used for approximating the number and capabilities of deployed naval assets.

Patrolling Behavior. We have implemented several of patrolling strategies, ranging from stationary reactive patrols to deliberative agents evaluating the situation in the assigned area and pro-actively deciding where to patrol and which vessels to protect. Naval vessel agents are controlled by a hierarchical structure of authority agents, reflecting the real-world chain-of-command. A central *Navy Authority* agent controls a set of *Task forces* (i.e. group of agents), each controlling a number of agents representing Naval vessels with on-board helicopters able to patrol the area and respond to attacks. More details can be found in [13].

3   Model Implementation

We have implemented the proposed multi-agent model in Java, employing selected components of the A-lite[6] simulation platform and using Google Earth for geo-referenced visualization. Scripts written in Groovy are used for scenario description. Below we describe the implementation of behavior models – see [13] for a detailed description of the (rest of) implementation.

The performance of the simulation is directly dependent on the number of agents (the most demanding are the pirate models). With approximately thousand vessels and one simulation step equal to 1 minute, our platform is able to simulate a month of real-world traffic in approximately one minute on a standard desktop computer (2.4Ghz, 4GB RAM, single-core use).

Agent Behavior Implementation. Behavior model implementation needs to be computationally efficient to allow simulation of thousands of vessel agents and expressive enough to model complex behavior and interactions between vessels. The agents should be able to execute multi-step plans while handling possible interruptions. Different vessels models share some behaviors – such as trajectory planning or basic pirate attack cycle – therefore re-usability should be supported. Moreover, to effectively implement adaptive pirates, we want to support learning directly in the behavior model implementation.

Extended finite state machines (FSM) fit the above requirements well. Individual states correspond to the principal mental states of the vessel agent (such as move, attack, hijacked, patrol etc.). Transitions between the states are defined by unconditional state transitions (a pair $\{s_{from}, s_{to}\}$, e.g. $\{wait, move\}$) or by conditional transitions triggered by external events (a tuple $\{s_{from}, event, s_{to}\}$, e.g. $\{move, shipSpottted, attack\}$). Each state stores its context when deactivated so that when reactivated, the context can be restored to continue the previously interrupted plan. Transitions between states can be internally or externally triggered, thus allowing interruption of plans or actions. FSMs are easily extensible and state implementations can be easily reused. It is possible to create abstract skeletons of various FSM and then enrich them with specific behaviors. The ability to learn can be implemented using internal state variables.

The problem of incorporating time into FSMs is solved by allocating the agent each turn a time quantum which the agent uses for performing the activity associated with its current state. Concurrent actions are not supported by our FSM implementation but this is not required for the level of modeling used.

Agent Interaction. The agents can interact in two ways: (1) by exchanging messages (cooperative interaction) or (2) by forcing the other agent to transit between states by triggering an external environmental event. The first option is used for communication between merchant vessels transiting in a group or between task-forces (i.e. exchange of information); the latter is used for non-voluntary interactions, e.g. when a pirate hijacks a merchant vessel or when a helicopter disables a pirate vessel and prevents it from attacking.

---

[6] http://agents.felk.cvut.cz/projects/#alite

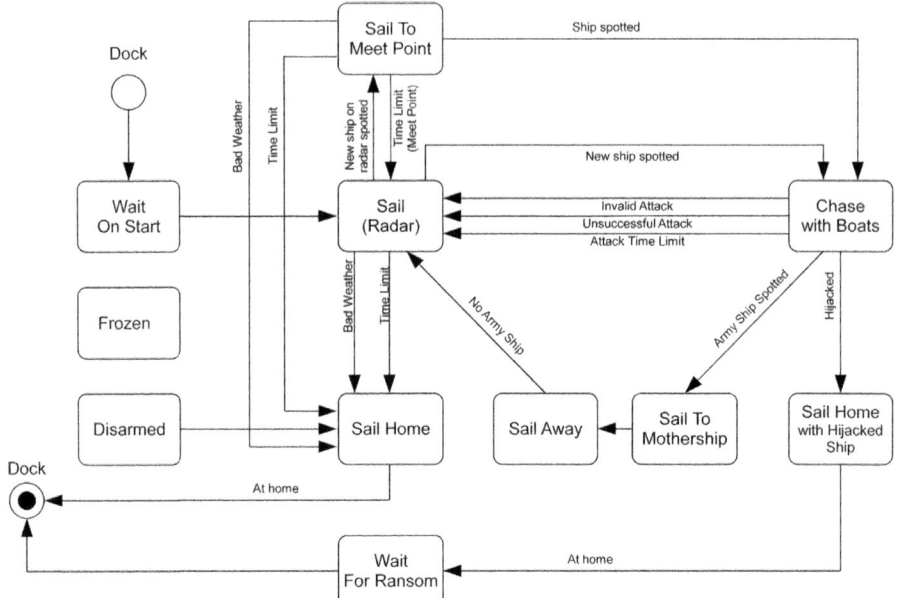

Fig. 4. FSM implementing the behavior of a pirate with a mothership and a radar

Pirate FSM Example. Figure 4 depicts a FSM of a pirate equipped with a radar and a mothership. The pirate waits an arbitrary amount of time in its home port and then sails into the open sea, scanning with the radar for a potential target. If it detects a merchant vessel, it approaches it and launches attack. If the attack is successful and the pirate vessel hijacks the vessel, it gains full control over the vessel and forces it to go to its home port and wait for the payment of ransom.

There are several external events that can disrupt this cycle: the pirate has limited resources, thus the amount of time to spend at sea – when this amount is depleted, the pirate has to return back to its home port. If a naval vessel is spotted, the agent interrupts its chase and moves away from the naval vessel. The forced state transition can be triggered by the naval vessel when it intercepts pirate attack. First, the pirate is *disabled* by a helicopter and later *disarmed* by a warship. The unconditioned state transition ($\{disarmed, sailHome\}$) then returns the control to the pirate agent, which then sails to its home port.

4   Model Validation

To validate the proposed model, we compare simulation output with real-world data. We first validate the model of merchant vessels alone and then look at the full model. We only employ visual comparison at the moment; formal statistical comparison will be part of our future work.

4.1   Long-Range Shipping Traffic Model Validation

To verify the accuracy of merchant traffic, we compare the traces of simulated merchant vessels with the aggregated AIS-based maritime shipping density map [9] (gathered from 2005 till the beginning of 2008, see Figure 5a). A few differences are visible (see Figure 5). (1) Main corridors are narrower in the simulation. This difference could be removed by adding perturbations to simulated vessel routes. (2) The simulated traces do not exactly correspond to the corridors near the Socotra island. This difference is caused by the introduction of the IRTC corridor which is not yet reflected in the density map (our traces are more up-to-date). (3) The routes along the Somali coast extend farther from the coast in the simulated data. Again, the routing in these waters underwent major changes in the last years and the density map does not yet fully reflects the tendency of vessels to stay farther from the dangerous Somali coast. Our model uses a risk-based planner which takes this factor into consideration.

The reference data [9] also contain samples of trajectories of vessels not considered in our simulation, such as fishing vessels, maritime-research vessels or private vessels. These samples account for the irregular traffic outside the main corridors.

Overall the agreement between the real and simulated traffic is very good. In the future, we aim to introduce and evaluate a formal measure of model accuracy.

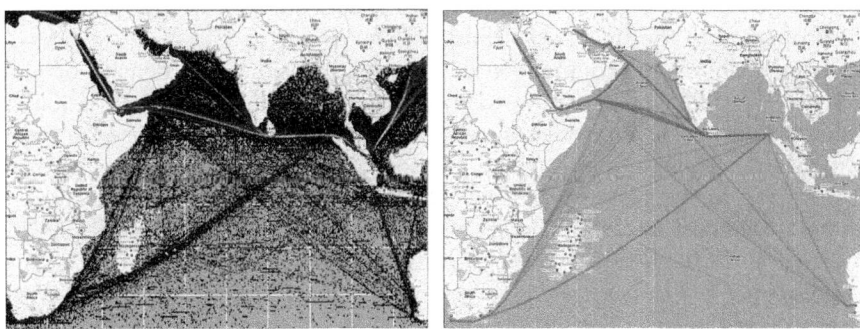

(a) Real-world ship density (2005-2008).   (b) Simulated merchant vessel traffic.

Fig. 5. Comparison of the real-world shipping density (left) and simulated merchant vessel traffic (right)

4.2   Piracy Model Validation

Due to the lack of real-world pirate movement data, we are not able to directly validate pirate behavior models. Instead we compare the pirate attack density, as produced by the pirate models in conjunction with the models of merchant and navy vessels, and compare this density with the data provided by IMB Piracy Reporting Centre (see Section 2.2).

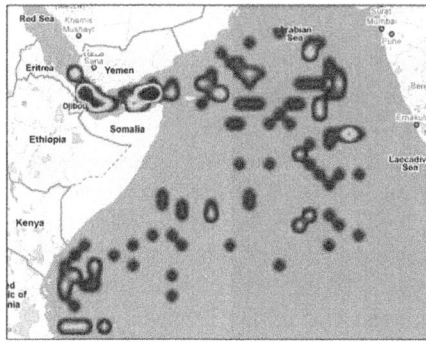 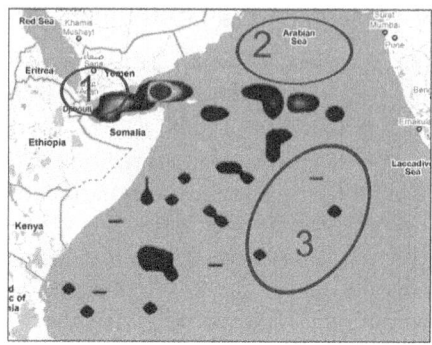

(a) Real pirate attack density for 2010.   (b) Simulated attack density for a 1-year period.

Fig. 6. Comparison of real and simulated attack densities for a 1-year period

For comparison, we have simulated one year of merchant vessel traffic through the region with realistic traffic density (approximately 60 vessels a day in IRTC). We do not have any estimates of real-world density of pirates in the area. We have therefore set their number so that the overall number of incidents corresponds to the number observed in the real-world. We have simulated 15 pirates – 5 simple, 5 radar equipped pirates and 5 pirates with a mothership and a radar. Finally, we have placed 3 naval task forces, each equipped with 2 warships and a helicopter, into the IRTC according to the 4W grid.

Figure 6 shows the comparison of the real and simulated density of pirate attacks. The red circles denote main differences in incident distribution. (1) Simulated pirates do not attack vessels in the Red Sea; this is because the current configuration focuses on the IRTC corridor. (2) There are no attacks in the Arabian Sea in the simulation. This is because the simulated pirates which sail far from the coast are equipped with a radar, and are thus almost always able to detect and attack vessels sailing in the shipping lane from the Gulf of Aden to Malaysia. (3) The density of attacks in the central Indian Ocean is lower; this is because of the lower density of the simulated merchant vessel traffic itself.

Overall, the agreement between the real-world and simulated pirate attack density is satisfactory, especially considering the random fluctuations in the real-world attack density and the fact that the simulated attack density is the result of the interaction of three types of vessels: merchant vessels, pirates and patrols. Each deviation in the behavior model is amplified through these interactions and can have a disproportional effect on the resulting incident density. After fixing the specific issues mentioned, the agreement between the model and reality should be further improved.

5   Group Transit Schedule Optimization

As an example application of the developed model, we use it to optimize the Gulf of Aden group transit scheme (introduced in Section 1.2). The current

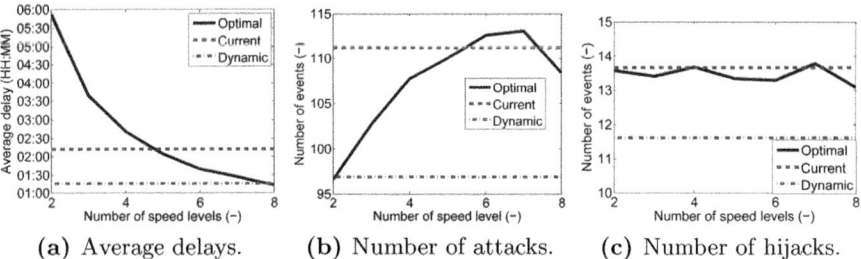

(a) Average delays.   (b) Number of attacks.   (c) Number of hijacks.

Fig. 7. Evaluation of different group transit schemes

group transit scheme uses fixed transit schedules designed to divide transiting vessels into five groups travelling at different speeds uniformly spaced between 10 and 18 knots. Our motivation is to explore whether the number of attacks and the transit delay caused by participating in group transit can be reduced by (1) proposing a different set of speed levels for the fixed-schedule scheme and (2) employing a dynamic grouping scheme, which takes into account not only the speeds of transiting vessels but their time of arrival too.

Optimal Fixed Schedule Group Transit. The real-world distribution of merchant vessel speeds is approximated by a histogram (see Figure 8) with bins of a fixed width (can be set e.g. to 0.1, 0.5 or 1 knot). The optimization problem can be formulated as partitioning the histogram into N groups, corresponding to group transit speeds, which minimize the average transit delay (i.e. the delay caused by traveling at a group speed which might be lower than the vessel's normal cruising speed).

Dynamic Group Transit. Instead of assigning vessels to groups according to predefined schedules and speed levels, dynamic grouping forms groups on the fly. This allows to form groups that better reflect actual arrival times and speed distribution of incoming vessels, at the expense of a more complex coordination scheme required. Our current implementation uses a greedy technique which assigns incoming vessels with similar speeds to the same group (see [13] for details).

Evaluation. We have used the simulation to evaluate the average transit delay (Figure 7a), the average number of transit groups and the number of total and successful pirate attacks for different grouping schemes. Figure 8 shows the optimal speed levels for the fixed-schedule group transit with 5 speed levels. Note that in contrast to the current scheme, new speed levels are not distributed uniformly and are concentrated around the mean vessel speed. As shown in Table 2, new speed levels result in shorter transit times and a lower average number of transit groups, thus potentially saving millions of US dollars.

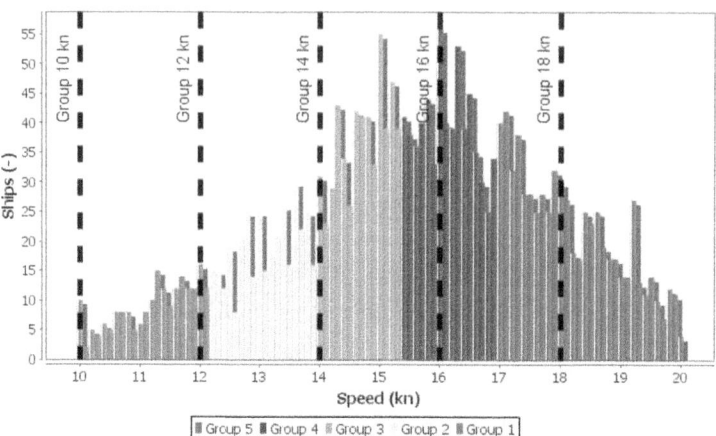

Fig. 8. Vessel speed histogram and its optimum partitioning into 5 speed groups

Table 2. Time savings and average number of transit groups for selected grouping schemes. ΔT is the average transit time reduction compared to the current scheme (per one transit and aggregated for all transits in one year). The overall savings are computed as $(\Delta T/year) \cdot \$30000$ (according to [6]).

Scheme	Schedule	ΔT/ship	ΔT/year	Avg. groups	Savings
current	$\{10, 12, 14, 16, 18\}$	0 min	0 days	10.73	-
opt. 5	$\{10, 12.2, 14, 15.4, 17\}$	7 min	97 days	9.16	2.9m USD
opt. 6	$\{10, 11.7, 13.3, 14.6, 16, 17.6\}$	31 min	430 days	9.88	12.9m USD
dynamic	-	56 min	778 days	12.14	23.4m USD

The grouping for 6 speed levels further reduces group transit delay and saves over a year of total vessel travel time. The number of pirate incidents does not significantly vary with the increasing number of speed levels (see Figures 7b, 7c), because even though there are potentially more groups to attack, the speed of the groups is higher on average. The dynamic scheme is by far the most efficient in reducing transit delay although at the expense of higher number of groups (i.e. smaller average group size).

6   Conclusion

Multi-agent simulations have a great potential for designing and evaluating solutions to a range of issues in international shipping, including the threat of contemporary maritime piracy. To this end, we have developed a first fully agent-based model of global traffic that accounts for the effects of maritime piracy on global shipping. The model is based on a range of real-world datasets and represents the operation of three types of vessels and their interactions. Despite the lack of hard data on some phenomena related to maritime piracy, the implemented model shows good correspondence in areas where validation data are available. As an example of potential applications of the developed model, we have shown how it can be used to optimize the current Gulf of Aden group transit scheme.

Overall, the implemented model demonstrates the viability of agent-based modeling in the maritime domain and opens a number of promising research directions.

As the immediate next step, we plan to improve the validation of our proposed model by employing statistical measures of model error and by considering the model dynamics too, in particular the ability to properly capture the co-evolution of merchant and pirate strategies over time. In a longer term, we aim to leverage some of the recent economic studies of piracy (e.g. [1]) in order to endogenize selected parameters of the model (in particular the intensity of pirate attacks) by calculating what economic incentives, survival risks and alternative livelihoods pirates face.

Acknowledgments. Funded by the Office of Naval Research (grant no. N000140 910537), by the American Science Information Center AMVIS (grant no. LH11051), and by the Czech Ministry of Education, Youth and Sports under grant "Decision Making and Control for Manufacturing III" (grant no. MSM 6840770038).

References

1. The economics of piracy – pirate ransoms and livelihoods off the coast of Somalia. Technical report, GeoPolicity (2011),
   http://www.geopolicity.com/upload/content/pub_1305229189_regular.pdf
2. Bernhardt, K.: Agent-based modeling in transportation. Artificial Intelligence in Transportation E-C113, 72–80 (2007)
3. Bourdon, S., Gauthier, Y., Greiss, J.: MATRICS: A Maritime Traffic Simulation. Technical report, Defence R&D Canada (2007)
4. Bošanský, B., Lisý, V., Jakob, M., Pěchouček, M.: Computing time-dependent policies for patrolling games with mobile targets. In: Proceedings of the International Conference on Autonomous Agents and Multiagent Systems (2011)
5. CAPT George McGuire, R.: Combined maritime forces (cmf) - who we are and wider military counter piracy update, 12 (2009),
   http://www.cusnc.navy.mil/marlo/Events/DEC-MARLO-DubaiConference_files -2009/CAPT%20McGuire.ppt
6. Elbeck, M., Tirtiroglu, E.: The threat of piracy on maritime transportation. International Journal of Society Systems Science 2(2), 125–133 (2010)
7. Expedition. Somalia pirate attacks, 4 (2008),
   http://bbs.keyhole.com/ubb/ubbthreads.php?ubb=showflat&Number=1242871 &site_id=1
8. Gilpin, R.: Counting the Costs of Somali Piracy. Technical report, US Institute of Peace (2009)
9. Halpern, B.S., Walbridge, S., Selkoe, K.A., Kappel, C.V., Micheli, F., D'Agrosa, C., Bruno, J.F., Casey, K.S., Ebert, C., Fox, H.E.: A global map of human impact on marine ecosystems. Science 319(5865), 948 (2008)

10. Hasegawa, K., Hata, K., Shioji, M., Niwa, K., Mori, S., Fukuda, H.: Maritime Traffic Simulation in Congested Waterways and Its Applications. In: Proceedings of the 4th Conference for New Ship and Marine Technology (New S-Tech 2004), Chine, pp. 195–199 (2004)

11. ICC Commercial Crime Services. Hostage-taking at sea rises to record levels, says IMB (2010),
    http://www.icc-ccs.org/news/429-hostage-taking-at-sea-rises-to-record-levels-says-imb

12. Jain, M., Kardes, E., Kiekintveld, C., Ordonez, F., Tambe, M.: Security Games with Arbitrary Schedules: A Branch and Price Approach. In: Proceedings of the Conference on Artificial Intelligence (2010)

13. Jakob, M., Vaněk, O., Bošanský, B., Hrstka, O., Pěchouček, M.: Adversarial modeling and reasoning in the maritime domain year 2 report. Technical report, ATG, CTU, Prague (2010)

14. Krajzewicz, D., Hertkorn, G., Rössel, C., Wagner, P.: Sumo (simulation of urban mobility) – an open-source traffic simulation. In: MESM 2002 (2002)

15. Köse, E., Basar, E., Demirci, E., Güneroglu, A., Erkebay, S.: Simulation of marine traffic in istanbul strait. Simulation Modelling Practice and Theory 11(7-8), 597–608 (2003)

16. Lozano-Perez, T., Wesley, M.A.: An algorithm for planning collision-free paths among polyhedral obstacles. Communication of the ACM (1979)

17. MSCHOA. Gulf of aden internationally recommended transit corridor and group transit explanation (August 2010),
    http://www.shipping.nato.int/GroupTrans1/file/_WFS/GroupTransit12aug2010.pdf

18. Pěchouček, M., Šišlák, D.: Agent-based approach to free-flight planning, control, and simulation. IEEE Intelligent Systems 24(1), 14–17 (2009)

19. Sundaram, R.K.: Studies in Choice and Welfare. Springer, Heidelberg (2005)

20. Vaněk, O., Jakob, M., Lisý, V., Bošanský, B., Pěchouček, M.: Iterative game-theoretic route selection for hostile area transit and patrolling. In: Proccedings of the International Conference on Autonomous Agents and Multiagent Systems (2011)

How to Do Social Simulation in Logic: Modelling the Segregation Game in a Dynamic Logic of Assignments

Benoit Gaudou, Andreas Herzig, Emiliano Lorini, and Christophe Sibertin-Blanc

University of Toulouse, France
UMR 5505, Institut de Recherche en Informatique de Toulouse (IRIT), CNRS, France
IRIT, Université Paul Sabatier, 118 Route de Narbonne, F-31062 TOULOUSE CEDEX 9
{benoit.gaudou,christophe.sibertin-blanc}@univ-tlse1.fr,
{emiliano.lorini,andreas.herzig}@irit.fr

Abstract. The aim of this paper is to show how to do social simulation in logic. In order to meet this objective we present a dynamic logic with assignments, tests, sequential and nondeterministic composition, and bounded and non-bounded iteration. We show that our logic allows to represent and reason about a paradigmatic example of social simulation: Schelling's segregation game. We also build a bridge between social simulation and planning. In particular, we show that the problem of checking whether a given property P (such as segregation) will emerge after n simulation moves is nothing but the planning problem with horizon n, which is widely studied in AI: the problem of verifying whether there exists a plan of length at most n ensuring that a given goal will be achieved.

1 Introduction

In a recent debate Edmonds [9] attacked what he saw as "empty formal logic papers without any results" that are proposed in the field of multi-agent systems (MASs). He opposed them to papers describing social simulations: according to Edmonds the latter present many experimental results which are useful to better understand social phenomena, while the former kind of papers only aim at studying some relevant concepts and their mathematical properties (axiomatization, decidability, etc.), while not adding anything new to our understanding of social phenomena. In response to Edmonds's attack, some researchers defended the use of logic in MAS in general, and in particular in *agent-based social simulation* (ABSS) [10,5,7]. For example, in [5] it is argued that logic is relevant for MAS because it can be used to construct a much needed formal social theory. In [10] it is argued that logic can be useful in ABSS because a logical analysis based on (a) a philosophical or sociological theory, (b) observations and data about a particular social phenomenon, and (c) intuitions — or a blend of them — can be considered to provide the requirements and the specification for an ABSS system and more generally a MAS. Moreover, a logical system might help to check the validity of the ABSS model and to adjust it by way of having a clear understanding of the formal model underpinning it. All these researchers consider logic and ABSS not only as compatible, but also as complementary methodologies.

D. Villatoro, J. Sabater-Mir, and J.S. Sichman (Eds.): MABS 2011, LNAI 7124, pp. 59–73, 2012.

The idea we defend in this paper is much more radical than those of the above advocates of logic-based approaches. Our aim is to show that ABSS can be directly done in logic and that a logical specification of a given social phenomenon can be conceived as an ABSS model of this phenomenon. We believe that the use of adequate theorem provers will allow to obtain results that are beyond the possibilities of existing simulators. As a first step towards our aim we present in this paper a simple logic called DL-PA (Dynamic Logic of Propositional Assignments). DL-PA is an extension of propositional logic with dynamic operators. These operators allow to reason about *assignments* $p\leftarrow\top$ and $p\leftarrow\bot$ changing the truth value of a propositional variable p to 'true' or 'false' and about *tests* $\Phi?$ of the truth of a Boolean formula Φ. More generally, DL-PA allows to reason about those facts that will be true after complex events π that are built from assignments and tests by means of the operators of sequential composition $(\pi_1; \pi_2)$, nondeterministic composition $(\pi_1\cup\pi_2)$, bounded iteration $(\pi^{\leq n})$, and unbounded iteration $(\pi^{<\infty})$.

In order to illustrate the power of our logic we show that a paradigmatic ABSS model can be represented in our logic: Schelling's segregation game [17]. The problem of checking whether (under some initial conditions) a given property P such as segregation will *possibly emerge* after n simulation moves is reduced to the problem of checking in our logic whether the initial conditions imply that formula φ encoding property P will be true at the end of at least one sequence of events π of length at most n. Similarly, the problem of checking whether P will *necessarily emerge* after n simulation moves is reduced to the problem of checking whether the initial conditions imply that φ will be true at the end of every sequence of events π of length n. Actually the latter is nothing but the planning problem with horizon n, which is widely studied in AI and is for example at the base of the state of the art planner SatPlan [15]: the problem of verifying whether there exists a plan of length at most n ensuring that a given goal φ will be achieved. In the general case this problem is known to be in PSPACE, *i.e.* decidable in polynomial space [3]. We show that our logic fits these boundaries. In the past such PSPACE hard decision problems were considered to be out of reach of automated theorem provers. However, in the last 20 years huge progress was made on that kind of problems: state-of-the-art theorem provers for PSPACE complete problems were shown to be of practical interest in particular in semantic web applications even for realistic problem instances with thousands of clauses [14].

One might wish to go beyond the simple existential and universal quantifications that we mentioned above. This can be achieved by means of modal operators with counting (stemming from graded modal logics [11,21] and description logics [1]). We briefly discuss this extension of DL-PA and show that complexity of the star-free fragment remains in PSPACE.

Simulation and logic use quite different terminologies. Table 1 summarizes the correspondences between the concepts used in simulation and those used in logic. Note that the term 'model' occurs in both terminologies, but has different meanings: in simulation a model stands for a formal or conceptual model of a particular application one wishes to investigate, such as Schelling's segregation game in our case; in DL-PA, a model of a formula is a valuation where that formula is true.[1] A further difference between both fields is that logical formulas allow to talk about the whole search space (e.g. about what may necessarily emerges in all paths through the space of possible paths), while simulation is only about a single path in the search space.

Table 1. Terminologies in simulation and in logic

simulation	dynamic logic
model	logical language + domain laws
state	state, valuation (in DL-PA also called a model)
individual action	atomic event, atomic program
simulation step	complex event, complex program
property	logical formula
state has a property	valuation is a model of a formula
model has a property	domain laws imply formula
simulation engine	theorem prover

The rest of the paper is organized as follows. In Section 2 we describe the segregation game. In Section 3 we define our basic logic, and in Section 4 we show how it allows to reason about the segregation game. Finally we sketch some extensions (Section 5) and conclude (Section 6).[2]

2   The Segregation Game

In this section we give an informal description of the segregation game. A formal description is given in Section 4.

2.1   The Original Model

Thomas C. Schelling in [17] studied the phenomenon of segregation and in particular the conditions of its occurrence due to "discriminatory individual choices" in groups with recognizable distinctions such as sex, age, colour, etc. The best-known example is

---

[1] The identification of a model with a valuation is therefore just as in propositional logic, and is proper to our logic DL-PA (and more generally to logics of propositional control). The kind of models that are used in standard dynamic and temporal logics are more complex transition systems having a set of possible worlds, a transition relation between possible worlds, and a valuation for each possible worlds.

[2] In the MABS pre-proceedings version of this article we gave a more general PSPACE complexity result for the whole DL-PA, but the proof turned out to be incorrect. We conjecture that the problem of DL-PA model checking (allowing for formulas with the $\pi^{<\infty}$ operator) is in fact EXPTIME hard. Specific solvers exist for problems in this complexity class, but they are much less efficient than those for PSPACE problems. We thus chose to consider only the star-free fragment of DL-PA in this paper.

the formation of color-dependent residential areas, under the influence of the individual preference of being surrounded by at most a threshold number of neighbours with different colour: above the threshold inhabitants are unhappy and will move to another location.

One of the main results of Schelling's work is to show that the segregation phenomenon emerges even with a quite high tolerance threshold. For example, even if each inhabitant accepts that the majority of the neighbours surrounding him has a colour different from his, there will nevertheless be a tendency to form groups of inhabitants with the same colour.

2.2 The Implemented Model

The segregation model has been implemented in many languages and formalisms, in particular in almost all agent-based simulation platforms. Good examples are NetLogo [24,23] and GAMA [19]. Two mains implementations have been proposed for this model: cellular automaton models (where the cells are the active entities) and agent-based models (where inhabitants are represented as agents and can move from one cell to another). We represent here the Segregation model as a cellular automaton and will discuss in the conclusion how to model the agent-based version.

The global environment of the simulation is taken as a chessboard-like grid $N \times N$. Each of its cells is represented by a couple of integers $(k, l) \in [1..N] \times [1..N]$. A cell is either red (inhabited by a red agent), or blue (inhabited by a blue agent), or has no colour (uninhabited). When an unhappy inhabitant moves from one place to another free one then the latter takes the colour of the former and the former becomes colourless.

The two main parameters of the simulation are:

– the number of inhabitants $|\mathbb{A}|$ and
– the tolerance threshold: the number of different inhabitants from which on an inhabitant is unhappy, which is supposed to be the same for every inhabitant.

(Alternatively the parameters may be the density of inhabitants and the percentage of different inhabitants. We also note that most simulation models rather use the inverse of the tolerance threshold, called the similarity threshold.)

There is a scheduler which generates at each simulation step a random ordering of the set of cells and then activates the cells according to that ordering during the step. Upon activation a cell checks its happiness: a cell is happy iff the percentage of neighbour cells having a different colour is below its tolerance threshold. If the cell is unhappy then its inhabitant will move to another free cell on the grid.

The simulation stops when a stable state is reached. This is the case when every coloured cell (*i.e.* every inhabitant) is happy.

A simulation may have three different behaviours: (1) the simulation loops because the system does not reach a stable state where every cell is happy (typically when the density of inhabitants on the grid is high and the tolerance threshold is low, which means inhabitants are very intolerant); (2) the simulation stops but one cannot observe any kind of segregation (this is typically the case when the similarity threshold is very low, *i.e.* tolerance is high and/or density is very low); or (3) clusters of cells with the same colour emerge.

3 Dynamic Logic with Assignments

This section introduces the syntax and the semantics of the logic DL-PA. It is basically an instantiation of propositional dynamic logic PDL [13] with concrete programs $p\leftarrow\top$ and $p\leftarrow\bot$ assigning propositional variables to either true or false.

3.1 Language

We suppose given a countable set of propositional variables $\mathbb{P}$ with typical elements $p, q, \ldots$ Remember that the set of Boolean formulas of classical propositional logic can be built from $\mathbb{P}$ by means of the Boolean operators of negation and disjunction (the other connectives being defined by means of abbreviations).

For Schelling's game we will use evocative variables such as $R(k, l)$ and $B(k, l)$. Boolean formulas allow to express things such as $\bigwedge_{(k,l)} \neg(R(k, l) \wedge B(k, l))$, representing the fact that a cell cannot be both red and blue.

The set of *events* or *programs* Π is defined by the following BNF:

$$\pi ::= p\leftarrow\top \mid p\leftarrow\bot \mid \Phi? \mid \pi; \pi \mid \pi\cup\pi \mid \pi^{=n} \mid \pi^{\leq n} \mid \pi^{<\infty}$$

where p ranges over $\mathbb{P}$, Φ ranges over the set of Boolean formulas, and n ranges over the set of natural numbers $\mathbb{N}$.

The events $p\leftarrow\top$ and $p\leftarrow\bot$ are assignments modifying the truth value of the propositional variable p: the event $p\leftarrow\top$ sets p to true, and the event $p\leftarrow\bot$ sets p to false. $\Phi?$ is the test of Φ, which fails if Φ is false. $\pi_1; \pi_2$ denotes a sequence of events. $\pi^{=n}$ denotes iteration of π exactly n times, $\pi^{\leq n}$ denotes iteration of π up to n times, and $\pi^{<\infty}$ denotes arbitrary iteration of π. Assignments and tests are atomic events, while the other events are called complex. An example of a complex event is a blue inhabitant's move from location (k, l) to location (k', l'), written as the sequence $B(k, l)\leftarrow\bot; B(k', l')\leftarrow\top$.

The set of *formulas* $\mathcal{F}$ is defined by the following BNF:

$$\varphi ::= q \mid \top \mid \bot \mid \neg\varphi \mid \varphi \vee \varphi \mid \exists\pi. \varphi$$

where q ranges over $\mathbb{P}$ and π ranges over the set of events Π. (Observe that we use Φ for Boolean formulas and φ for formulas of DL-PA.) The formula $\exists\pi. \varphi$ reads "there is an execution of the event π after which φ is true". Hence $\exists\pi. \top$ has to be read "π may occur".

The operators '?', ';', '$\cup$' and '$^{<\infty}$' are familiar from propositional dynamic logic PDL. (We could as well use the Kleene star and write π^* instead of $\pi^{<\infty}$, as customary in PDL.) In uninterpreted PDL these operators combine abstract atomic programs, while in interpreted PDL they combine assignments of object variables to values from some domain. In contrast, atomic programs are here assignments of truth values to propositional variables, as previously studied in the dynamic epistemic logic literature [22,8,2].

The formula $\exists(q\leftarrow\top\cup q\leftarrow\bot). \varphi$ has the same interpretation as the quantified Boolean formula (QBF) $\exists q.\varphi$ [12]. The language of DL-PA can therefore be viewed as a generalisation of quantification over Boolean variables to complex 'quantification programs'.

The *length* of a formula φ, noted $|\varphi|$, is the number of symbols used to write down φ — without '$\langle$', '$\rangle$', dots, and parentheses —, where integers are supposed to have length 1.[3] For example

$$|\exists(q\leftarrow\top)^{\leq 3}.(q \vee r)| = 1 + |q\leftarrow\top| + 1 + 1 + |q \vee r| = 1 + 3 + 2 + 3 = 9.$$

The logical operators $\wedge$ and $\rightarrow$ are defined as abbreviations; for example $\varphi \rightarrow \psi$ abbreviates $\neg\varphi \vee \psi$. Moreover, $\forall\pi.\,\varphi$ abbreviates $\neg\exists\pi.\,\neg\varphi$. Hence $\forall\pi.\,\bot$ has to be read "π cannot occur". Familiar program constructions can also be defined as abbreviations: The skip event ('nothing happens') is defined as an abbreviation of $\top?$, and if φ then π_1 else π_2 is defined as an abbreviation of $(\varphi?;\pi_1)\cup(\neg\varphi?;\pi_2)$.

Remark 1. Note that could define programs π^k as abbreviations of the sequential composition of π, k times,[4] and then define $\pi^{\leq n}$ as abbreviations of $\bigcup_{0\leq k\leq n}\pi^k$. However, the expansion of these abbreviations would exponentially increase formula length. For the same reason we have avoided to introduce '$\leftrightarrow$' as an abbreviation.

We use τ as a placeholder for either $\top$ or $\bot$, and write $q\leftarrow\tau$ in order to talk about $q\leftarrow\top$ and $q\leftarrow\bot$ in an economic way.

3.2 Semantics

A *valuation* is nothing but a model of classical propositional logic, *viz.* a subset of the set of propositional variables $\mathbb{P}$.

A valuation V provides truth values for propositional variables. These truth values are modified by events: to each event π we associate a binary relation on valuations R_π that is inductively defined as follows:

$$
\begin{aligned}
R_{p\leftarrow\top} &= \{(V, V') \;:\; V' = V \cup \{p\}\} \\
R_{p\leftarrow\bot} &= \{(V, V') \;:\; V' = V \setminus \{p\}\} \\
R_{\pi_1;\pi_2} &= R_{\pi_1} \circ R_{\pi_2} \\
R_{\pi_1\cup\pi_2} &= R_{\pi_1} \cup R_{\pi_2} \\
R_{\varphi?} &= \{(V, V) \;:\; V \models \varphi\} \\
R_{\pi^{=n}} &= (R_\pi)^n \\
R_{\pi^{\leq n}} &= \bigcup_{0\leq m\leq n}(R_\pi)^m \\
R_{\pi^{<\infty}} &= \bigcup_{0\leq m}(R_\pi)^m
\end{aligned}
$$

We call the valuations V' such that $(V, V') \in R_\pi$ the *possible updates of V by* π. Observe that $R_{\top?}$ is indeed the 'nothing happens' event relating every valuation to itself.

Then the truth conditions are the usual ones for $\top$, $\bot$, negation and disjunction, plus one for $\exists\pi.\,\varphi$ in terms of possible updates:

$$
\begin{aligned}
&V \models p &&\text{iff } p \in V \\
&V \models \top && \\
&V \not\models \bot && \\
&V \models \neg\varphi &&\text{iff } V \not\models \varphi \\
&V \models \varphi \vee \psi &&\text{iff } V \models \varphi \text{ or } V \models \psi \\
&V \models \exists\pi.\,\varphi &&\text{iff there is } V' \text{ such that } V R_\pi V' \text{ and } V' \models \varphi
\end{aligned}
$$

---

[3] Precisely, the length of an integer n should be $\log n$. Our hypothesis is however without harm.
[4] The precise definition is inductive: $\pi^0 = $ skip, and $\pi^{k+1} = \pi^k;\pi$.

A valuation V is a *model of* φ if and only if $V \models \varphi$. A formula φ is satisfiable if and only if there exists a model of φ, and φ is valid if and only if every valuation is a model of φ.

3.3 Reduction Axioms for the Star-Free Fragment

The fragment of DL-PA without arbitrary iterations (called the 'star-free fragment' in PDL) can be axiomatised by means of reduction axioms. These axioms allow to eliminate all the dynamic operators from formulas. However, that elimination might result in an exponential blowup due to the operator of nondeterministic composition $\cup$. We will therefore later on characterize the complexity of validity checking by other means.

Proposition 1. *The following equivalences are* DL-PA *valid.*

$$\exists \pi^{=n}. \varphi \quad \leftrightarrow \quad \begin{cases} \varphi & \text{if } n = 0 \\ \exists \pi^{=n-1}. \exists \pi. \varphi & \text{if } n > 0 \end{cases}$$

$$\exists \pi^{\leq n}. \varphi \quad \leftrightarrow \quad \begin{cases} \varphi & \text{if } n = 0 \\ \exists \pi^{\leq n-1}. (\varphi \vee \exists \pi. \varphi) & \text{if } n > 0 \end{cases}$$

$$\exists \varphi?. \psi \quad \leftrightarrow \quad \varphi \wedge \psi$$

$$\exists \pi_1 \cup \pi_2. \varphi \quad \leftrightarrow \quad \exists \pi_1. \varphi \vee \exists \pi_2. \varphi$$

$$\exists \pi_1; \pi_2. \varphi \quad \leftrightarrow \quad \exists \pi_1. \exists \pi_2. \varphi$$

$$\exists p \leftarrow \tau. \neg \varphi \quad \leftrightarrow \quad \neg \exists p \leftarrow \tau. \varphi$$

$$\exists p \leftarrow \tau. (\varphi_1 \vee \varphi_2) \leftrightarrow \exists p \leftarrow \tau. \varphi_1 \vee \exists p \leftarrow \tau. \varphi_2$$

$$\exists p \leftarrow \tau. \top \quad \leftrightarrow \quad \top$$

$$\exists p \leftarrow \tau. \bot \quad \leftrightarrow \quad \bot$$

$$\exists p \leftarrow \tau. q \quad \leftrightarrow \quad \begin{cases} \tau & \text{if } q = p \\ q & \text{if } q \neq p \end{cases}$$

These equivalences provide a complete set of reduction axioms for ∞-free dynamic operators $\exists \pi$. Call red the mapping on DL-PA formulas which iteratively applies the above equivalences from the left to the right, starting from one of the innermost modal operators. It allows to first eliminate complex events, then push the dynamic operators inside the formula, and finally eliminate them when facing an atomic formula. For example, consider the complex formula $\exists p \leftarrow \bot^2. (p \vee q)$. First the complex event $p \leftarrow \bot^2$ is eliminated, then the innermost modal operator is distributed over $\vee$ and eliminated, and finally the outermost modal operator is distributed and eliminated:

$$\exists p \leftarrow \bot^2. (p \vee q) \leftrightarrow \exists p \leftarrow \bot. \exists p \leftarrow \bot. (p \vee q)$$
$$\leftrightarrow \exists p \leftarrow \bot. (\exists p \leftarrow \bot. p \vee \exists p \leftarrow \bot. q)$$
$$\leftrightarrow \exists p \leftarrow \bot. (\bot \vee q)$$
$$\leftrightarrow \exists p \leftarrow \bot. q$$
$$\leftrightarrow q$$

We have simplified a bit between the 3rd and 4th line, replacing the subformula $\bot \vee q$ by the equivalent q.

Proposition 2. *Let φ be a formula in the language of* DL-PA *without the arbitrary iteration operator $\pi^{<\infty}$. Then*

1. red(φ) *has no modal operators;*
2. red(φ) $\leftrightarrow \varphi$ *is* DL-PA *valid;*
3. red(φ) *is* DL-PA *valid iff* red(φ) *is valid in classical propositional logic.*

Proposition 2 indicates a close relationship between star-free DL-PA and propositional logic. The merit of former over the latter is to provide a model theory and an intuitive and more succinct language. Both are valuable from a modelling perspective.

3.4 Complexity for the Star-Free Fragment

Proposition 2 tells us that star-free DL-PA is not more expressive than classical propositional logic. However, reduction may exponentially increase the length of the formula because of the event operators $\cup$ and $\pi^{\leq n}$. But this is a suboptimal procedure, as we shall see now.

We first give the complexity result for model checking. The inputs of the model checking problem are a valuation V and a formula φ, and the problem is to decide whether $V \models \varphi$.

Theorem 1. *The problem of star-free* DL-PA *model checking is PSPACE-complete.*
PROOF. We first establish *hardness* by reducing the problem of validity of QBFs to star-free DL-PA model checking. Consider a fully quantified Boolean formula

$$\Phi = \exists q_1 \forall q_2 \exists q_3 \ldots \exists q_{m-1} \forall q_m. \varphi$$

where $m \geq 0$ is even and where $\varphi(q_1, \ldots, q_m)$ is a propositional formula containing no variables other than $q_1, \ldots, q_m$. (The hypothesis that the number of quantifiers is even is without loss of generality: it suffices to add a dummy variable q_m not occurring in φ.) We define

$$\Phi^{\text{DL-PA}} = \exists \pi_1. \forall \pi_2. \ldots \exists \pi_{m-1}. \forall \pi_m. \varphi$$

where $\pi_k = q_k \leftarrow \top \cup q_k \leftarrow \bot$, for $1 \leq k \leq m$. Consider the valuation over the set $\mathbb{P} = \{q_1, \ldots, q_m\}$ of propositional variables such that, say, $V(q_i) = \text{ff}$ for all q_i. It is readily checked that Φ is valid in Quantified Boolean Logic iff $\Phi^{\text{DL-PA}}$ is true in V. Since both the size of $\Phi^{\text{DL-PA}}$ and the size of the model are linear in the size of Φ, we conclude that free-star DL-PA model checking is PSPACE-hard.

Proof of *membership* requires a recursive definition of the set of sequences of atomic events *admitted* by a complex event π.

$$
\begin{aligned}
adm(p \leftarrow \tau) &= \{p \leftarrow \tau\} \\
adm(\Phi?) &= \{\Phi?\} \\
adm(\pi_1; \pi_2) &= \{\alpha_1; \alpha_2 \; : \; \alpha_1 \in adm(\pi_1) \text{ and } \alpha_2 \in adm(\pi_2)\} \\
adm(\pi_1 \cup \pi_2) &= adm(\pi_1) \cup adm(\pi_2) \\
adm(\pi^{=0}) &= \{\top?\} \\
adm(\pi^{=n+1}) &= \{\alpha_1; \alpha_2 \; : \; \alpha_1 \in adm(\pi^{=n}) \text{ and } \alpha_2 \in adm(\pi)\} \\
adm(\pi^{\leq 0}) &= \{\top?\} \\
adm(\pi^{\leq n+1}) &= adm(\pi^{\leq n}) \cup \\
&\quad \{\alpha_1; \alpha_2 \; : \; \alpha_1 \in adm(\pi^{\leq n}) \text{ and } \alpha_2 \in adm(\pi)\}
\end{aligned}
$$

The main point in the proof is that every possible update of a valuation V by a complex event π can also be reached by a sequence of atomic events that is admitted by π and that is at most as long as π. Based on that one can prove that membership of a couple of valuations (V, V') in R_π can be decided in polynomial space. Finally one can prove that a formula φ can be evaluated in space polynomial in the size of φ.   ∎

Theorem 2. *The problem of star-free DL-PA validity checking is PSPACE-complete.*

PROOF. Hardness can be proved by translating QBF formulas to star-free DL-PA in the same way as in Theorem 1. Membership can be proved for the star-free DL-PA satisfiability checking problem as follows: given φ we guess a model V. (V can be supposed to be of polynomial size because we may restrict our attention to the propositional variables occurring in φ, and neglect those that don't.) Then we check whether $V \models \varphi$, which can be done in polynomial space by mirroring the truth conditions. This shows that star-free DL-PA satisfiability can be checked in NPSPACE. Now by Savitch's theorem NPSPACE = PSPACE, and therefore star-free DL-PA satisfiability can be checked in polynomial space. It follows that the complementary star-free DL-PA validity problem can be checked in polynomial space, too.   ∎

The above result shows that DL-PA is *more succinct* than propositional logic: there are DL-PA formulas (and even star-free DL-PA formulas) such that every equivalent propositional formula is exponential longer.

4   The Segregation Game in DL-PA

In Section 2 we introduced Schelling's segregation game in an informal way. Let us now model it in DL-PA as a cellular automaton. We start by describing agents whose tolerance threshold is 0.

4.1   Propositional Variables

We need three kinds of propositional variables:

$R(k, l)$ "cell (k, l) is red"
$B(k, l)$ "cell (k, l) is blue"
$Done(k, l)$ "it was already cell (k, l)'s turn in the present step"

where every (k, l) is a location in the grid $[1..N] \times [1..N]$. The following abbreviations will be useful:

$$NB_{<1}(k, l) \overset{\text{def}}{=} \bigwedge_{k', l' \leq N \,:\, |k'-k|, |l'-l| \leq 1} \neg B(k', l')$$

$$NR_{<1}(k, l) \overset{\text{def}}{=} \bigwedge_{k', l' \leq N \,:\, |k'-k|, |l'-l| \leq 1} \neg R(k', l')$$

$$UnH_{<1}(k, l) \overset{\text{def}}{=} (R(k, l) \wedge \neg NB_{<1}(k, l)) \vee (B(k, l) \wedge \neg NR_{<1}(k, l))$$

$$Free(k, l) \overset{\text{def}}{=} \neg R(k, l) \wedge \neg B(k, l)$$

$$Segreg_{<1} \overset{\text{def}}{=} \neg \bigvee_{k,l} UnH_{<1}(k, l)$$

$NB_{<1}(k, l)$ can be read "location (k, l) has no blue neighbour" and similarly for $NR_{<1}(k, l)$. $UnH_{<1}(i, k, l)$ can be read "location (k, l) is inhabited and has some neighbour with a different colour". $Free(k, l)$ can be read "location (k, l) is free". Finally, the property of segregation holds —noted $Segreg_{<1}$— if and only if "every inhabitant has no neighbour with a different colour".

Let us compute the length of these formulas. The length of both $NB_{<1}(k, l)$ and $NR_{<1}(k, l)$ is in $O(1)$, *i.e.* it is constant (the quantification over the locations (k', l') being void because there are exactly eight neighbour locations of (k, l)). The same holds for the length of $\neg UnH_{<1}(k, l)$. Finally, the length of $Segreg_{<1}$ is in $O(N^2)$.

4.2 Describing Inhabitants' Moves

The move of an inhabitant from a location (k, l) to the location (k', l') is modelled by the swap of color between cells (k, l) and (k', l'). It can be described by a complex event in our language of events.

$$move(k, l) \overset{def}{=} \bigcup_{k', l'} (\neg B(k', l') \land \neg R(k', l'))? ;$$
$$((B(k, l)? ; B(k, l) \leftarrow \bot ; B(k', l') \leftarrow \top) \cup$$
$$(R(k, l)? ; R(k, l) \leftarrow \bot ; R(k', l') \leftarrow \top))$$

Then a move of the simulation is described by a nondeterministic composition of agent moves (plus some turn taking management):

$$move \overset{def}{=} \left(\bigcup_{k,l} \neg Done(k, l)?; (UnH_{<1}(k, l)?; move(k, l)) \cup \neg UnH_{<1}(k, l)?); Done(k, l) \leftarrow \top \right) ;$$
$$\left(((\bigwedge_{k,l} Done(k, l))? ; initialize) \cup (\neg \bigwedge_{k,l} Done(k, l))? \right)$$

Using if-then-else this can be written in a way that is perhaps more understandable as:

$$move \overset{def}{=} \left(\bigcup_{k,l} \neg Done(k, l)?; (if\ UnH_{<1}(k, l)\ then\ move(k, l)\ else\ skip) ; Done(k, l) \leftarrow \top \right) ;$$
$$\left(if\ (\bigwedge_{k,l} Done(k, l))\ then\ initialize\ else\ skip \right)$$

The initialize event starts a new simulation step, setting the $Done(k, l)$ variables of the inhabited cells to false: after it, none of the inhabited cells has played yet.

$$initialize \overset{def}{=} (B(k_1, l_1) \lor R(k_1, l_1))? ; Done(k_n, l_n) \leftarrow \bot ; \dots ;$$
$$(B(k_n, l_n) \lor R(k_n, l_n))? ; Done(k_n, l_n) \leftarrow \bot$$

Nondeterministic choice of a location in the move formula corresponds to the scheduler in simulation platforms such as NetLogo or GAMA. The latter generates at the beginning of each step a random ordering of the set of agents and then activates the agents according to that ordering during the step. A simulation step consists in N^2 executions of move.

The lengths of both $move(k, l)$ and initialize are in $O(N^2)$. The length of move is in $O(N^2 \times N^2) = O(N^4)$.

4.3 Initial State

In order to properly analyse the segregation model, we must describe the *initial state* in our formalism:

$$\text{Init} = \left(\bigwedge\nolimits_{(k,l)\in J_R} \text{R}(k,l) \right) \wedge \left(\bigwedge\nolimits_{(k,l)\in J_B} \text{B}(k,l) \right) \wedge \left(\bigwedge\nolimits_{(k,l)\in J_R \cup J_B} \neg\text{Done}(k,l) \right)$$

where $J_R \subseteq N^2$ is the set of red cells and $J_B \subseteq N^2$ the set of blue cells. As a cell cannot be blue and red these two sets have to be disjoint, *i.e.* we require that $J_R \cap J_B = \emptyset$. Moreover, the numbers of colored cells must be smaller than the total number of cells: $|J_R| + |J_B| \leq N^2$. Finally, note that we do not say anything about the status of uninhabited cells: we do not care whether $\text{Done}(k,l)$ is true or false there. The length of Init is in $O(N^2)$.

4.4 Describing and Proving Properties

Properties to be maintained (invariants). During the execution of a simulation, several properties should be maintained and thus be always true. In the case of Schelling's game, a cell cannot be both red and blue:

$$\chi_1 = \bigwedge\nolimits_{k,l} \neg (\text{B}(k,l) \wedge \text{R}(k,l))$$

We need an auxiliary definition which expresses that at least n individuals have property P:

$$\text{atleast}\,(n,P) = \left(\bigvee_{(k_1,l_1),\dots,(k_n,l_n)\,:\,(k_i,l_i)\neq(k_j,l_j)\text{ if }i\neq j} P(k_1,l_1) \wedge \dots \wedge P(k_n,l_n) \right)$$

This allows us to state that the numbers of red and blue cells are exactly $|J_R|$ and $|J_B|$ just as in the initial state:

$$\chi_2 = \text{atleast}\,(|J_R|,\text{R}) \wedge \neg\text{atleast}\,(|J_R|+1,\text{R}) \wedge \text{atleast}\,(|J_B|,\text{B}) \wedge \neg\text{atleast}\,(|J_B|+1,\text{B})$$

Together these formulas make up the invariants of Schelling's game:

$$\text{Invs} = \chi_1 \wedge \chi_2$$

The length of χ_1 is in $O(N^2)$, while that of χ_2 is in $O(2^{N^2})$ (which means that will be is costly to check the latter property).

The difference between Init and Invs is that while Init has just to be true in the initial state, the laws must be true in the initial state and in any update of the current state. In order to ensure that our modelling works properly the first things to do is to check that the invariants hold verified in the initial state and are then preserved by any sequence of events from move. In order to prove this it suffices to prove that the formulas

$$\text{Init} \rightarrow \text{Invs}$$
$$\text{Invs} \rightarrow \forall \text{move}. \text{Invs}$$

are both DL-PA valid. From this it follows by standard principles of modal logic that $\text{Invs} \rightarrow \forall \text{move}^n. \text{Invs}$ and $\text{Invs} \rightarrow \forall \text{move}^{\leq n}. \text{Invs}$ are DL-PA valid.

Properties to be achieved. In our language we can express things such as "segregation *will always* occur after n moves" (φ_1), "segregation *may* occur within n moves" (φ_2), "when segregation occurs then none of the agents will move" (φ_3), etc.:

$$\varphi_1 = \forall\mathsf{move}^{=n}.\,\mathsf{Segreg}_{<1}$$
$$\varphi_2 = \exists\mathsf{move}^{\leq n}.\,\mathsf{Segreg}_{<1}$$
$$\varphi_3 = \mathsf{Segreg}_{<1} \rightarrow \forall\mathsf{move}.\,\bot$$

Other kinds of properties will be discussed in Section 5.

Given a property described by a formula φ, what we are interested in is to check whether the formula

$$\mathsf{Init} \rightarrow \varphi$$

is DL-PA valid, where φ is one of the above properties.

It is important to note that the lengths of the formulas $\mathsf{Segreg}_{<1}$, $\neg\mathsf{UnH}_{<1}(k, l)$, Init and of the complex event move are polynomial in the domain size parameter N; precisely, their maximum length is in $O(N^4)$. Therefore the length of the formulas $\mathsf{Init} \rightarrow \mathsf{Invs}$, $\mathsf{Invs} \rightarrow \forall\mathsf{move}.\mathsf{Invs}$ and $\mathsf{Init} \rightarrow \varphi_k$ is polynomial in N; precisely, their length is in $O(N^4)$. The validity problem in star-free DL-PA being in PSPACE we obtain the following results.

Proposition 3. *The validity of* $\mathsf{Init} \rightarrow \varphi_k$, *for* $\varphi_k \in \{\varphi_1, \varphi_2, \varphi_3\}$, *can be checked in space polynomial in* N.

We note that checking whether the invariants Invs hold is more expensive because of the combinatorial explosion in the expression of the constraint that the number of red and blue agents is constant.

All our decision problems being in PSPACE, we can envisage to use existing theorem provers for PSPACE problems to check the above properties, such as provers for modal logic K, for description logic ALC, or for Quantified Boolean Formulas. This requires a polynomial transformation of the formulas to be checked into the language of the respective logic.[5]

4.5   Varying the Inhabitants' Tolerance

The inhabitants modelled here are extremely intolerant. More tolerant inhabitants can be described as follows:

$$\mathsf{NB}_{<2}(k, l) \stackrel{\text{def}}{=} \bigwedge\nolimits_{(k_1, l_1),(k_2, l_2)\,:\,|k_1-k|,|l_1-l|,|k_2-k|,|l_2-l|\leq 1} \neg(\mathsf{B}(k_1, l_1) \wedge \mathsf{B}(k_2, l_2))$$
$$\mathsf{NB}_{<p}(k, l) \stackrel{\text{def}}{=} \bigwedge\nolimits_{(k_1, l_1),\dots,(k_p, l_p)\,:\,|k_m-k|,|l_m-l|\leq 1} \neg(\mathsf{B}(k_1, l_1) \wedge \dots \wedge \mathsf{B}(k_p, l_p))$$

$\mathsf{NB}_{<p}(k, l)$ is read "location (k, l) has less than p blue neighbours". $\mathsf{NR}_{<p}(k, l)$ is defined accordingly. $\mathsf{UnH}_{<1}(k, l)$ and $\mathsf{Segreg}_{<1}$ can be generalised to $\mathsf{UnH}_{<p}(k, l)$ and $\mathsf{Segreg}_{<p}$ in the obvious way. One may also stipulate that an agent is happy if the percentage of agents in his neighbourhood with a colour different from his is below some threshold.

---

[5] While we know that such a transformation exists because all these problems are in the same complexity class, it remains to find an elegant such transformation.

For the same reason as for $NB_{<1}$, the length of $NB_{<2}$ and of any $NB_{<p}$ ($p \leq 8$) is in $O(1)$. It follows that the length of $UnH_{<2}(k, l)$ (and $UnH_{<p}(k, l)$) is still in $O(N^2)$, that of $Segreg_{<2}$ (and $Segreg_{<p}$) is still in $O(N^2)$, and that of move is still in $O(N^4)$. So complexity does not increase for these generalisations and just as in Section 4.4 such properties can still be checked in polynomial space.

5   More Expressive Languages

We now discuss some generalisations of our logic that allow to naturally express other properties one would like to check in simulations.

Let us introduce two new modal operators $\geq k\,\pi$ and $\geq \frac{1}{2}\,\pi$, where $\geq k\,\pi.\,\varphi$ reads "φ is true in at least k of the possible updates by π" and $\geq \frac{1}{2}\,\pi.\,\varphi$ reads "φ is true in most of the states after π". So the formula $\exists \pi.\,\varphi$ of Section 3 is nothing but $\geq 1\,\pi.\,\varphi$.

$$V \models \geq k\,\pi.\,\varphi \quad \text{iff} \quad |\{V' \;:\; (V, V') \in R_\pi \text{ and } V' \models \varphi\}| \geq k$$
$$V \models >\tfrac{1}{2}\,\pi.\,\varphi \quad \text{iff} \quad |\{V' \;:\; VR_\pi V' \;\&\; V' \models \varphi\}| > |\{V' \;:\; VR_\pi V' \;\&\; V' \not\models \varphi\}|$$

This allows to formulate interesting properties of segregation game such as:

– "segregation will occur within n moves *at least k times*" (ψ_1);
– "segregation will occur within n moves *exactly k times*" (ψ_2);
– "segregation will occur after n moves in most of the cases" (ψ_3).

In formulas:

$$\psi_1 = \geq k\ \mathsf{move}^{\leq n}.\ Segreg_{<p}$$
$$\psi_2 = \geq k\ \mathsf{move}^{\leq n}.\ Segreg_{<p} \wedge \neg \geq k{+}1\ \mathsf{move}^{\leq n}.\ Segreg_{<p}$$
$$\psi_3 = >\tfrac{1}{2}\ \mathsf{move}^{=n}.\ Segreg_{<p}$$

Model checking requires some more bookkeeping in order to count valuations, but can still be done in polynomial space. We obtain a PSPACE completeness result for the validity checking problem by using Savitch's theorem in the same way as we did in the proof of Theorem 2.

6   Conclusion

In this paper we have shown how to do social simulation in a dynamic logic with assignments, tests, sequential and nondeterministic composition, and bounded and non-bounded iteration. In Section 5 we have shown that our logic allows to study interesting properties of segregation game. For instance, it allows to test whether, given a certain initial configuration of the grid, segregation will emerge at some point in the future at least k times (or exactly k times). In order to test such properties by standard simulation methods it would be necessary to run several computer simulations and to then perform a statistical analysis of the results that have been observed. This allows then to estimate the frequency with which segregation emerges at some point of the simulation. In this sense, the approach proposed in this work offers a novel method for social simulation studies and analysis. We have started to implement the segregation game in QBF provers [6].

In this paper, we focused on a cellular automaton version of the segregation model. We did so in order to reduce the length of our formulas describing the segregation game. We present now a sketch of formalization of the agent-based model in order to illustrate the possible use of our logic not only in cellular automaton-based simulations but also in agent-based simulations. In the agent-based version of the model, every inhabitant would be represented by an individual (typically noted $i, j, \dots$) who is situated on a grid cell that is described by its coordinates (k, l). Each of these agents can move on the grid from one cell to another one. Each agent is characterized by his colour (*e.g.* red or blue) and his location on the grid. We thus have to adapt the propositional variables in order to take into account this new representation. We do so by introducing $At(i, k, l)$ variables expressing that agent i is at location (k, l). The variables $R(k, l)$ and $Done(k, l)$ will be changed to $R(i)$ and $Done(i)$, because agents and no more cells will have a color and perform actions. The simulation will stop when every agent is happy ($UnH_{<1}(k, l)$ will thus become $UnH_{<1}(i, k, l)$). This new formalization will induce a noticeable increase of complexity of some of our formulas; for example, the length of the formula move is currently in $O(N^4)$, while it will be in $O(N^{22})$ in the agent version when we take the parameter $p = 8$. Nevertheless, the possibility to represent an agent-based simulation model in our logic opens us much more possibilities of interesting applications.

Instead of our logic we could also have used other logical approaches to reasoning about actions such as the Situation Calculus [16], the Fluent Calculus [20], or the Event Calculus [18]. However, while these formalisms allow to represent more or less the same things, their mathematical analysis is less developed: while there are some decidability results, there are no complexity results that could be compared to the PSPACE completeness result for our logic.

As we have said in the introduction the kind of properties we want to prove can be viewed as finite horizon planning problems. To witness, the way we prove our PSPACE complexity results matches *e.g.* the Chapman's TWEAK [4]. We could therefore have used existing finite horizon planners in order to prove properties of simulations. It has to be noted that planners typically build plans, while we are only interested in proving plan existence. However, it is an interesting research avenue to exploit a possible convergence of the fields of simulation and planning.

Acknowledgements. We wish to thank Philippe Balbiani and Charles Cultien for their useful comments on the complexity aspects of DL-PA and on the logical modeling of the segregation game. This work was partially supported by the French RTRA STAE project MAELIA.

References

1. Baader, F., Calvanese, D., McGuinness, D.L., Nardi, D., Patel-Schneider, P.F. (eds.): Description Logic Handbook. Cambridge University Press (2003)
2. van Benthem, J., van Eijck, J., Kooi, B.: Logics of communication and change. Information and Computation 204, 1620–1662 (2006)
3. Bylander, T.: The computational complexity of propositional strips planning. Artificial Intelligence 69, 165–204 (1994)

4. Chapman, D.: Planning for conjunctive goals. Artificial Intelligence 32(3), 333–377 (1987)
5. Conte, R., Paolucci, M.: Responsibility for societies of agents. Journal of Artificial Societies and Social Simulation 7(4) (2004)
6. Cultien, C.: Implementing dynamic logic of propositional assignments in a QBF solver. Master's thesis, Université de Toulouse (September 2011)
7. Dignum, F., Edmonds, B., Sonenberg, L.: Editorial: The Use of Logic in Agent-Based Social Simulation. Journal of Artificial Societies and Social Simulation 7(4) (2004)
8. van Ditmarsch, H.P., van der Hoek, W., Kooi, B.: Dynamic epistemic logic with assignment. In: Proceedings of AAMAS 2005, pp. 141–148. ACM Press (2005)
9. Edmonds, B.: How Formal Logic Can Fail to Be Useful for Modelling or Designing MAS. In: Lindemann, G., Moldt, D., Paolucci, M. (eds.) RASTA 2002. LNCS (LNAI), vol. 2934, pp. 1–15. Springer, Heidelberg (2004)
10. Fasli, M.: Formal systems and agent-based social simulation equals null? Journal of Artificial Societies and Social Simulation 7(4) (2004)
11. Fattorosi-Barnaba, M., de Caro, F.: Graded modalities I. Studia Logica 44, 197–221 (1985)
12. Garey, M.R., Johnson, D.S.: Computers and Intractability: A Guide to the Theory of NP-Completeness. W. H. Freeman Co. (1979)
13. Harel, D., Kozen, D., Tiuryn, J.: Dynamic Logic. MIT Press, Cambridge (2000)
14. Horrocks, I.: Using an expressive description logic: Fact or fiction? In: Proceedings of KR 1998, pp. 636–649 (1998)
15. Kautz, H.A., Selman, B.: Planning as satisfiability. In: Proceedings of ECAI 1992, pp. 359–363 (1992)
16. Reiter, R.: Knowledge in Action: Logical Foundations for Specifying and Implementing Dynamical Systems. MIT Press (2001)
17. Schelling, T.C.: Dynamic Models of Segregation. Journal of Mathematical Sociology 1, 143–186 (1971)
18. Shanahan, M.: Solving the frame problem: a mathematical investigation of the common sense law of inertia. MIT Press (1997)
19. Taillandier, P., Drogoul, A., Vo, D.A., Amouroux, E.: GAMA: a simulation platform that integrates geographical information data, agent-based modeling and multi-scale control. In: Proceedings of PRIMA 2010 (2010)
20. Thielscher, M.: The logic of dynamic systems. In: Proceedings of the 14th International Joint Conference on Artificial Intelligence (IJCAI 1995), Montreal, Canada, pp. 1956–1962 (1995)
21. van der Hoek, W.: On the semantics of graded modalities. Journal of Applied Non-Classical Logics 2(1) (1992)
22. van Eijck, J.: Making things happen. Studia Logica 66(1), 41–58 (2000)
23. Wilensky, U.: Netlogo segregation model. Technical report, Center for Connected Learning and Computer-Based Modeling. Northwestern University, Evanston, IL (1997)
24. Wilensky, U.: Netlogo. Technical report, Center for Connected Learning and Computer-Based Modeling. Northwestern University, Evanston, IL (1999)

An Agent-Based Proxemic Model for Pedestrian and Group Dynamics: Motivations and First Experiments

Lorenza Manenti[1,2], Sara Manzoni[1,2], Giuseppe Vizzari[1,2],
Kazumichi Ohtsuka[3], and Kenichiro Shimura[3]

[1] Complex Systems and Artificial Intelligence (CSAI) Research Center
Department of Computer Science, Systems and Communication (DISCo)
University of Milan - Bicocca, Viale Sarca 336/14, 20126 Milano, Italy
{manenti,manzoni,vizzari}@disco.unimib.it
[2] Crystals Project, Center of Research Excellence in Hajj and Omrah (Hajjcore)
Umm Al-Qura University, Makkah, Saudi Arabia
[3] Research Center for Advanced Science & Technology, The University of Tokyo, Japan
tukacyf@mail.ecc.u-tokyo.ac.jp, shimura@tokai.t.u-tokyo.ac.jp

Abstract. The simulation of pedestrian dynamics is a consolidated area of application for agent-based models: successful case studies can be found in the literature and off-the-shelf simulators are commonly employed by end-users, decision makers and consultancy companies. These models, however, generally neglect or treat in a simplistic way aspects like (i) the impact of cultural heterogeneity among individuals and (ii) the effects of the presence of groups and particular relationships among pedestrians. This work is aimed, on one hand, at introducing some fundamental anthropological considerations on which most pedestrian models are based, and in particular Edward T. Hall's work on proxemics. On the other hand, the paper describes an agent-based model encapsulating in the pedestrian's behavioural model effects representing both proxemics and a simplified account of influences related to the presence of groups in the crowd. The model is tested in a simple scenario to evaluate the implications of some modeling choices and the presence of groups in the simulated scenario. Results are discussed and compared to experimental observations and to data available in the literature.

Keywords: crowd modeling and simulation, agent-based models.

1 Introduction

There are several features of crowds of pedestrians suggesting that they can be considered as complex entities: the mix of competition for the space shared by pedestrians and the collaboration due to the (not necessarily explicit but generally shared) social norms, the dependency of individual choices on the past actions of other individuals and on the current perceived state of the system, the possibility to detect self-organization and emergent phenomena they are all indicators of the intrinsic complexity of a crowd. The relevance of human behaviour, and especially of the movements of pedestrians, in built environment in normal and extraordinary situations, and its implications for the activities of architects, designers and urban planners are apparent (see, e.g., [7] and [41]), especially considering dramatic episodes such as terrorist attacks, riots and fires, but

D. Villatoro, J. Sabater-Mir, and J.S. Sichman (Eds.): MABS 2011, LNAI 7124, pp. 74–89, 2012.
© Springer-Verlag Berlin Heidelberg 2012

also due to the growing issues in facing the organization and management of public events (ceremonies, races, carnivals, concerts, parties/social gatherings, and so on) and in designing naturally crowded places (e.g. stations, arenas, airports). Computational models for the simulation of crowds are thus growingly investigated in the scientific context, and these efforts led to the realization of commercial off-the-shelf simulators often adopted by firms and decision makers[1]. Even if research on this topic is still quite lively and far from a complete understanding of the complex phenomena related to crowds of pedestrians in the environment, models and simulators have shown their usefulness in supporting architectural designers and urban planners in their decisions by creating the possibility to envision the behaviour/movement of crowds of pedestrians in specific designs/environments, to elaborate what-if scenarios and evaluate their decisions with reference to specific metrics and criteria.

A Multi-Agent Systems (MAS) approach to the modeling and simulation of complex systems has been applied in very different contexts, from the study of social systems [2], to biology (see, e.g., [13]), and it is considered one of the most successful types of applications of agent–based computing [23], even if this approach is still relatively young, compared, for instance, to analytical equation-based modeling. The MAS approach has also been adopted in the pedestrian and crowd modeling context, especially due to the expressiveness of the approach, that is particularly suited to the definition of models in which autonomous and possibly heterogeneous agents can be defined, situated in an environment, provided with the possibility to perceive it, decide and try to carry out the most appropriate line of action, possibly interacting with other agents as well as the environment itself. The approach can lead to the definition of models that are richer and more expressive than other approaches that were traditionally adopted in the modeling of pedestrians, that respectively consider pedestrians as particles subject to forces (see, e.g., [19]), in physical approaches, or particular states of cells in which the environment is subdivided, in CA approaches (see, e.g., [35,9]).

The main aim of this work is to present the motivations, fundamental research questions and directions, and some preliminary results of an agent–based modeling and simulation approach to the multidisciplinary investigation of the complex dynamics that characterize aggregations of pedestrians and crowds. This work is set in the context of the Crystals project[2], a joint research effort between the Complex Systems and Artificial Intelligence research center of the University of Milano–Bicocca, the Centre of Research Excellence in Hajj and Omrah and the Research Center for Advanced Science and Technology of the University of Tokyo. The main focus of the project is on the adoption of an agent-based pedestrian and crowd modeling approach to investigate meaningful relationships between the contributions of anthropology, cultural characteristics and existing results on the research on crowd dynamics, and how the presence of heterogeneous groups influence emergent dynamics in the context of the Hajj and Omrah. The last point is in fact an open topic in the context of pedestrian modeling and simulation approaches [1]: the implications of particular relationships among

---

[1] See, e.g., Legion Ltd. (http://www.legion.com), Crowd Dynamics Ltd. (http://www.crowddynamics.com/), Savannah Simulations AG (http://www.savannah-simulations.ch).

[2] http://www.csai.disco.unimib.it/CSAI/CRYSTALS/

pedestrians in a crowd are generally not considered or treated in a very simplistic way by current approaches. In the specific context of the Hajj, the yearly pilgrimage to Mecca that involves over 2 millions of people coming from over 150 countries, the presence of groups (possibly characterized by an internal structure) and the cultural differences among pedestrians represent two fundamental features of the reference scenario. Studying implications of these basic features is the main aim of the Crystals project.

The paper breaks down as follows: after a the following section introduces the current state of the art in the modeling and simulation of pedestrian dynamics. Section 3 describes some basic anthropological and sociological theories that were selected to describe the phenomenologies that will be considered in the agent-based model definition. Section 4 briefly describes a model encompassing basic anthropological rules for the interpretation of mutual distances by agents and basic rules for the cohesion of groups of pedestrians, while Sect. 5 summarizes the results of the application of this model in a simple simulation scenario. Conclusions and future developments end the paper.

2   Related Works

It is not a simple task to provide a compact yet comprehensive overview of the different approaches and models for the representation and simulation of crowd dynamics. In fact, entire scientific interdisciplinary workshops and conferences are focused on this topic (see, e.g., the proceedings of the first edition of the International Conference on Pedestrian and Evacuation Dynamics [37] and consider that this event has reached the fifth edition in 2010). However, most approaches can be classified according to the way pedestrians are represented and managed, and in particular: (i) pedestrians as *particles subject to forces* of attraction/repulsion, (ii) pedestrians as particular *states of cells in a CA*, (iii) pedestrians as *autonomous agents*, situated in an environment.

2.1   Particle–Based Approach

Several models for pedestrian dynamics are based on an analytical approach, representing pedestrian as particles subject to forces, modeling the interaction between pedestrian and the environment (and also among pedestrians themselves, in the case of *active walker* models [20]). Forces of attraction lead the pedestrians/particles towards their destinations (modeling thus their goals), while forces of repulsion are used to represent the tendency to stay at a distance from other points of the environment. This kind of effect was introduced by a relevant and successful example of this modeling approach, the *social force* model [19]; this approach introduces the notion of social force, representing the tendency of pedestrians to stay at a certain distance one from another; other relevant approaches take inspiration from fluid-dynamic [18] and magnetic forces [29] for the representation of mechanisms governing flows of pedestrians.

While this approach is based on a precise methodology and has provided relevant results, it represents pedestrian as mere particles, whose goals, characteristics and interactions must be represented through equations, and it is not simple thus to incorporate heterogeneity and complex pedestrian behaviours in this kind of model.

2.2 Cellular Automata Approach

A different approach to crowd modeling is characterized by the adoption of Cellular Automata (CA), with a discrete spatial representation and discrete time-steps, to represent the simulated environment and the entities it comprises. The cellular space includes thus both a representation of the environment and an indication of its state, in terms of occupancy of the sites it is divided into, by static obstacles as well as human beings. Transition rules must be defined in order to specify the evolution of every cell's state; they are based on the concept of neighborhood of a cell, a specific set of cells whose state will be considered in the computation of its transition rule. The transition rule, in this kind of model, generates the illusion of movement, that is mapped to a coordinated change of cells state. To make a simple example, an atomic step of a pedestrian is realized through the change of state of two cells, the first characterized by an *"occupied"* state that becomes *"vacant"*, and an adjacent one that was previously *"vacant"* and that becomes *"occupied"*. This kind of application of CA-based models is essentially based on previous works adopting the same approach for traffic simulation [27].

Local cell interactions are thus the uniform (and only) way to represent the motion of an individual in the space (and the choice of the destination of every movement step). The sequential application of this rule to the whole cell space may bring to emergent effects and collective behaviours. Relevant examples of crowd collective behaviours that were modeled through CAs are the formation of lanes in bidirectional pedestrian flows [9], the resolution of conflicts in multidirectional crossing pedestrian flows [10]. In this kind of example, different states of the cells represent pedestrians moving towards different exits; this particular state activates a particular branch of the transition rule causing the transition of the related pedestrian to the direction associated to that particular state. Additional branches of the transition rule manage conflicts in the movement of pedestrians, for instance through changes of lanes in case of pedestrians that would occupy the same cell coming from opposite directions.

It must be noted, however, that the potential need to represent goal driven behaviours (i.e. the desire to reach a certain position in space) has often led to extend the basic CA model to include features and mechanisms breaking the strictly locality principle. A relevant example of this kind of development is represented by a CA based approach to pedestrian dynamics in evacuation configurations [35]. In this case, the cellular structure of the environment is also characterized by a predefined desirability level, associated to each cell, that, combined with more dynamic effects generated by the passage of other pedestrians, guide the transition of states associated to pedestrians. Recent developments of this approach introduce even more sophisticated behavioural elements for pedestrians, considering the anticipation of the movements of other pedestrians, especially in counter flows scenarios [28].

2.3 Autonomous Agents Approach

Recent developments in this line of research (e.g. [21,14]), introduce modifications to the basic CA approach that are so deep that the resulting models can be considered much more similar to agent–based and Multi Agent Systems (MAS) models exploiting a cellular space representing spatial aspects of agents' environment. A MAS is a system made up of a set of autonomous components which interact, for instance according to collaboration or competition schemes, in order to contribute in realizing an overall behaviour that could not be generated by single entities by themselves. As previously introduced, MAS models have been successfully applied to the modeling and simulation of several situations characterized by the presence of autonomous entities whose action and interaction determines the evolution of the system, and they are growingly adopted also to model crowds of pedestrians [7,15,39,3]. All these approaches are characterized by the fact that the agents encapsulate some form of behaviour inspired by the above described approaches, that is, forms of attractions/repulsion generated by points of interest or reference in the environment but also by other pedestrians.

Some of the agent based approaches to the modeling of pedestrians and crowds were developed with the primary goal of providing a realistic 3D visualization of the simulated dynamics: in this case, the notion of realism includes elements that are considered irrelevant by some of the previous approaches, and it does not necessarily require the models to be validated against data observed in real or experimental situations. The approach described in [26] and in [38] is characterized by a very composite model of pedestrian behaviour, including basic reactive behaviours as well as a cognitive control layer; moreover, actions available to agents are not strictly related to their movement, but they also allow forms of direct interaction among pedestrians and interaction with objects situated in the environment. Other approaches in this area (see, e.g., [30]) also define layered architectures including cognitive models for the coordination of composite actions for the manipulation of objects present in the environment. Another relevant approach, described in [25], is less focused on visual effectiveness of the simulation dynamics, and it supports a flexible definition of the simulation scenario also without requiring the intervention of a computer programmer. However, these virtual reality focused approaches to pedestrian and crowd simulation were not tested in paradigmatic case studies, modeled adopting analytical approaches or cellular automata and validated against real data.

It is worth mentioning that another paper of this volume also deals with issues related to the validation of pedestrian simulation results, and in particular on how to gather substantial amount of data about pedestrian movement [31].

3   Interdisciplinary Approach

Pedestrian and crowd modeling research context regards events in which a large number of people may be gathered or bound to move in a limited area; this can lead to serious safety and security issues for the participants and the organizers. The understanding of the dynamics of large groups of people is very important in the design and management of any type of public events. In addition to safety and security concerns also the comfort of event participants is another aim of the organizers and managers of crowd related events. Large people gatherings in public spaces (like pop-rock concerts or religious rites participation) represent scenarios in which crowd dynamics can be quite complex due to different factors (the large number and heterogeneity of participants, their interactions, their relationship with the performing artists and also exogenous factors like dangerous situations and any kind of different stimuli present in the environment [36]). The traditional and current trend in social sciences studying crowds is still characterized by a non-dominant behavioral theory on individuals and crowds dynamics, although it is recognized that a behavioural theory is needed to improve the current state of the art in pedestrian and crowd modeling and simulation [22].

3.1 Proxemics

The term *proxemics* was first introduced by Hall with respect to the study of set of measurable distances between people as they interact [17]. In his studies, Hall carried out analysis of different situations in order to recognize behavioral patterns. These patterns are based on people's culture as they appear at different levels of awareness. In [16] Hall proposed a system for the notation of proxemic behavior in order to collect data and information on people sharing a common space. Hall defined proxemic behavior and four types of perceived distances: *intimate distance* for embracing, touching or whispering; *personal distance* for interactions among good friends or family members; *social distance* for interactions among acquaintances; *public distance* used for public speaking. Perceived distances depend on some additional elements which characterize relationships and interactions between people: posture and sex identifiers, sociofugal-sociopetal (SFP) axis, kinesthetic factor, touching code, visual code, thermal code, olfactory code and voice loudness.

   Proxemic behavior includes different aspects which could it be useful and interesting to integrate in crowd and pedestrian dynamics simulation. In particular, the most significant of these aspects being the existence of two kinds of distance: *physical* distance and *perceived* distance. While the first depends on physical position associated to each person, the latter depends on proxemic behavior based on culture and social rules.

   It must be noted that some recent research effort was aimed at evaluating the impact of proxemics and cultural differences on the fundamental diagram [12], a typical way of evaluating both real crowding situations and simulation results. Moreover, a first attempt to explicitly include proxemic considerations not only as a background element in the motivations a behavioural model is based upon, but rather as a concrete element of the model itself [40].

3.2 Crowds: Canetti's Theory

Elias Canetti's work [11] proposes a classification and an ontological description of the crowd; it represents the result of 40 years of empirical observations and studies from psychological and anthropological viewpoints. Elias Canetti can be considered as belonging to the tradition of social studies that refer to the crowd as an entity dominated by uniform moods and feelings. We preferred this work among others dealing with crowds due to its clear semantics and explicit reference to concepts of loss of individuality, crowd uniformity, spatio-temporal dynamics and *discharge* as a triggering entity generating the crowd, that could be fruitfully represented by computationally modeling approaches like MAS.

   The normal pedestrian behaviour, according to Canetti, is based upon what can be called the *fear to be touched* principle:

"There is nothing man fears more than the touch of the unknown. He wants to see what is reaching towards him, and to be able to recognize or at least classify it."
"All the distance which men place around themselves are dictated by this fear."

A discharge is a particular event, a situation, a specific context in which this principle is not valid anymore, since pedestrians are willing to accept being very close (within touch distance). Canetti provided an extensive categorization of the conditions, situations in which this happens and he also described the features of these situations and of the resulting types of crowds. Finally, Canetti also provides the concept of *crowd crystal*, a particular set of pedestrians which are part of a group willing to preserve its unity, despite crowd dynamics. Canetti's theory (and precisely the fear to be touched principle) is apparently compatible with Hall's proxemics, but it also provides additional concepts that are useful to describe phenomena that take place in several relevant crowding phenomena, especially from the Hajj perspective.

Recent developments aimed at formalizing, embedding and employing Canetti's crowd theory into computer systems (for instance supporting crowd profiling and modeling) can be found in the literature [6,4] and they represent a useful contribution to the present work. Moreover, additional recent works represent a relevant effort towards the modeling of groups, respectively in particle-based [24,42], in CA-based [34] and in agent-based approaches [32]: in all these approaches, groups are modeled by means of additional contributions to the overall pedestrian behaviour representing the tendency to stay close to other group members. However, some of the above approaches only deal with small groups in relatively low density conditions or they were not validated against real data.

4   An Agent-Based Proxemic Model

This section will describe a first step towards an agent–based model encompassing abstractions and mechanisms accounting based on fundamental considerations about proxemics and basic group behaviour in pedestrians. We first defined a very general and simple model for agents, their environment and interaction, then we realized a proof–of–concept prototype to have an immediate idea of the implications of our modeling choices.

The simulated environment represents a simplified real built environment, a corridor with two exits (North and South); later different experiments will be described with corridors of different size (10m wide and 20 m long as well as 5m wide and 10 m long). We represented this environment as a simple euclidean bi-dimensional space, that is discrete (meaning that coordinates are integer numbers) but not "discretized" (as in a CA). Pedestrians, in other words, are characterized by a position that is a pair $\langle x, y \rangle$ that does not not denote a cell but rather admissible coordinates in an euclidean space. Movement, the fundamental agent's action, is represented as a displacement in this space, i.e. a vector. The approach is essentially based on the Boids model [33], in which however rules have been modified to represent the phenomenologies described by the basic theories and contributions on pedestrian movement instead of flocks. The

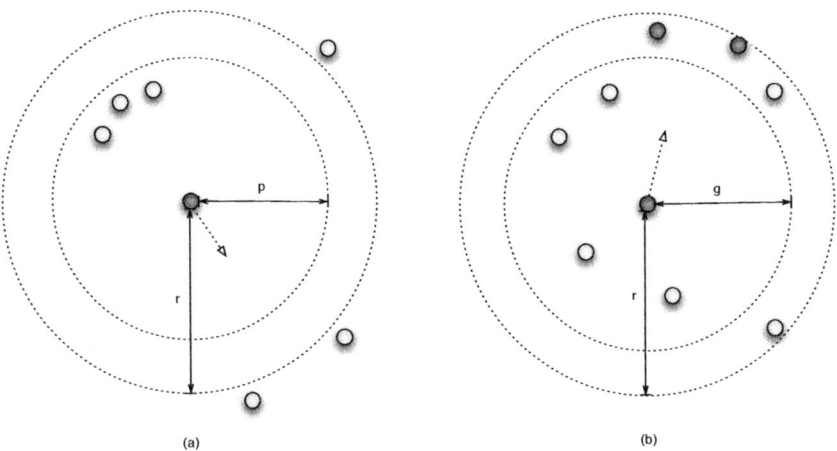

Fig. 1. Basic behavioural rules: a basic proxemic rule drives an agent to move away from other agents that entered/are present in his/her own personal space (delimited by the proxemic distance p) (a), whereas a member of a group will pursue members of his/her group that have moved/are located beyond a certain distance (g) but within his/her perception radius (r) (b).

main modifications are represented by the addition of a goal driven component, to direct pedestrian towards their destination in the environment, in addition to keeping an acceptable mutual distance, and by the removal of the alignment component.

Boundaries of the environment were defined: in the example Eastern and Western borders cannot be crossed and the movement of pedestrians is limited by the pedestrian position update function, which is an environmental responsibility. Every agent $a \in A$ (where A is the set of agents representing pedestrians of the modeled scenario) is characterized by a position pos_a represent by a pair of coordinates $\langle x_a, y_a \rangle$. Agent's action is thus represented by a vector $\overline{m}_a = \langle \delta_{x_a}, \delta_{y_a} \rangle$ where $|\overline{m}_a| = \sqrt{\delta_{x_a}^2 + \delta_{y_a}^2} < M$ where M is a parameter depending on the specific scenario representing the maximum displacement per time unit.

More complex environments could be modeled, for instance by means of a set of relevant objects in the scene, like points of interest but also obstacles. These objects could be perceived by agents according to their position and perceptual capabilities, and they could thus have implications on their movement. Objects can (but they do not necessarily must be) in fact be considered as attractive or repulsive by them. The effect of the perception of objects and other pedestrians, however, is part of agents' behavioural specifications. For this specific application, however, the perceptive capability of an agent a are simply defined as the set of other pedestrians that are present at the time of the perception in a circular portion of space or radius r_p centered at the current coordinates of agent a. In particular, each agent $a \in A$ is provided with a perception distance per_a; the set of perceived agents is defined as $P_a = p_1, \ldots, p_i$ where $d(a, i) = \sqrt{(x_a - x_i)^2 + (y_a - y_i)^2} \leq per_a$.

Pedestrians are modeled as agents situated in an environment, each occupying about 40 cm^2, characterized by a state representing individual properties. Their behaviour has a goal driven component, a preferred direction; in this specific example it does not change over time and according to agent's position in space (agents want to get out of the corridor from one of the exits, wither North or South), but it generally changes according to the position of the agent, generating a path of movement from its starting point to its own destination. The preferred direction is thus generally the result of a stochastic function possibly depending on time and current position of the agent. The goal driven component of the agent behavioural specification, however, is just one the different elements of the agent architectures that must include elements properly capturing elements related to general proxemic tendencies and group influence (at least), and we also added a small random contribution to the overall movement of pedestrians, as suggested by [8]. The actual layering of the modules contributing to the overall is object of current and future work. In the scenario, agents' goal driven behavioural component is instead rather simple: agents heading North (respectively South) have a deliberate contribution to their overall movement $\overline{m}_a^g = \langle 0, M \rangle$ (respectively $\overline{m}_a^g = \langle 0, -M \rangle$).

We realized a simulation scenario in a rapid prototyping framework[3] and we employed it to test the simple behavioural model that will be described in the following. In the realized simulator, the environment is responsible for updating the position of agents, actually triggering their action choice in a sequential way, in order to ensure fairness among agents. In particular, we set the turn duration to 100 ms and the maximum covered distance in one turn is 15 cm (i.e. the maximum velocity for a pedestrian is 1.5 m/s).

4.1 Basic Proxemic Rules

Every pedestrian is characterized by a culturally defined proxemic distance p; this value is in general related to the specific culture characterizing the individual, so the overall system is designed to be potentially heterogenous. In a normal situation, the pedestrian moves (according to his/her preferred direction) maintaining the minimum distance from the others above this threshold (rule *P1*). More precisely, for a given agent a this rule defines that the proxemic contribution to the overall agent movement $\overline{m}_a^p = 0$ if $\forall b \in P_a : d(a, b) \geq p$.

However, due to the overall system dynamics, the minimum distance between one pedestrian and another can drop below p. In this case, given a pedestrian a, we have that $\exists b \in P_a : d(a, b) < p$; the proxemic contribution to the overall movement of a will try to restore this condition (rule *P2*) (please notice that pedestrians might have different thresholds, so b might not be in a situation so that his/her P2 rule is activated). In particular, given $p_1, \dots, p_k \in P_a : d(a, p_i) < p$ for $1 \leq i \leq k$, given c the centroid of $pos_{p_1}, \dots, pos_{p_k}$, the proxemic contribution to the overall agent movement $\overline{m}_a^p = -k_p \cdot \overline{c - pos_a}$, where k_a is a parameter determining the intensity of the proxemic influence on the overall behaviour.

These basic considerations, also schematized in Fig. 1-A, lead to the definition of rules support a basic proxemic behaviour for pedestrian agents; these agents are not

---

[3] Nodebox – http://www.nodebox.org

characterized by any particular relationship binding them, with the exception of a shared goal, i.e. they are not a group but rather an unstructured set of pedestrians.

4.2 Group Dynamic Rules

We extended the behavioural specification of agents by means of an additional contribution representing the tendency of group members to stay close to each other. First of all, every pedestrian may be thus part of a group, that is, a set of pedestrians that mutually recognize their belonging to the same group and that are willing to preserve the group unity. This is clearly a very simplified, heterarchical notion of group, and in particular it does not account for hierarchical relationships in groups (e.g. leader and followers), but we wanted to start defining basic rules for the simplest form of group.

Every pedestrian is thus also characterized by a culturally defined proxemic distance g determining the way the pedestrian interprets the minimum distance from any other group member. In particular, in a normal situation a pedestrian moves (according to hie/her preferred direction and also considering the basic proxemic rules) keeping the maximum distance from the other members of the group below g (Rule *G1*). More precisely, for a given agent a, member of a group G, this rule defines that the group dynamic contribution to the overall agent movement $\overline{m}_a^g = 0$ if $\forall b \in \left(P_a \cap (G - \{a\})\right)$: $d(a, b) < g$.

However, due to the overall system dynamics, the maximum distance between one pedestrian and other members of his group can exceed g. In this case, the it will try to restore this condition by moving towards the group members he/she is able to perceive (rule *G2*). In particular, given $p_1, \ldots, p_k \in \left(P_a \cap (G - \{a\})\right)$: $d(a, p_i) \geq g$ for $1 \leq i \leq k$, given c the centroid of $pos_{p_1}, \ldots, pos_{p_k}$, the proxemic contribution to the overall agent movement $\overline{m}_a^g = k_g \cdot \overline{c - pos_a}$, where k_a is a parameter determining the intensity of the group dynamic influence on the overall behaviour.

This basic idea of group influence on pedestrian dynamics, also schematized in Fig. 1-B, lead to the extension of the basic proxemic behaviour for pedestrian agents of the previous example. We tested the newly defined rules in a similar scenario but including groups of pedestrians. In particular, two scenarios were analyzed. In the first one, we simply substituted 4 individual pedestrians in the previous scenario with a group of 4 pedestrians. The group was able to preserve its unity in all the tests we conducted, but the average travel time for the group members actually increased. Individuals, in other words, trade some of their potential speed to preserve the unity of the group. In a different scenario, we included 10 pedestrians and a group of 4 pedestrians heading North, 10 pedestrians and a group of 4 pedestrians heading South. In this circumstances, the two groups sometimes face and they are generally able to find a way to form two lanes, actually avoiding each other. However, the overall travel time for group members actually increases in many of the simulations we conducted.

In Fig. 2 two screenshots the of the prototype of the simulation system that was briefly introduced here. Individual agents, those that are not part of a group, are depicted in blue, but those for which rule P2 is activated (they are afraid to be touched) turn to orange, to highlight the invasion of their personal space. Members of groups are depicted in violet and pink. The two screenshots show how two groups directly facing

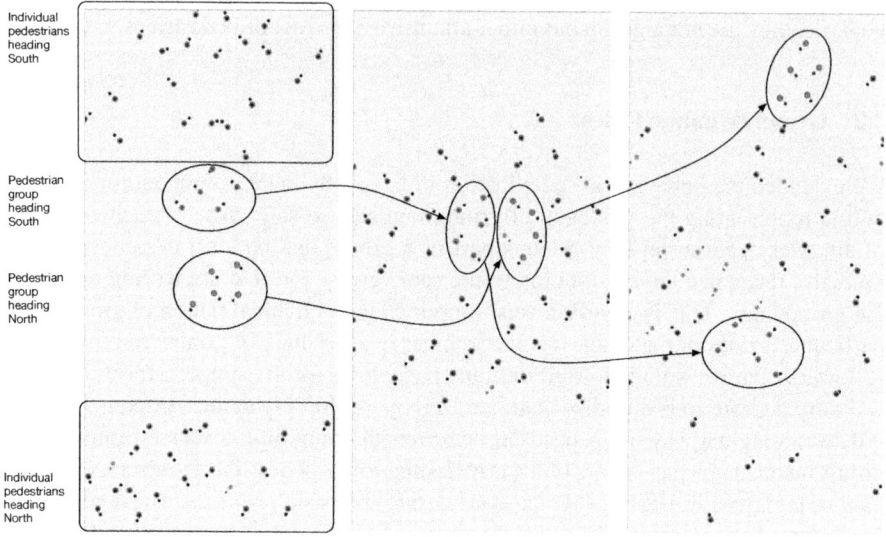

Fig. 2. Screenshots of the prototype of the simulation system

each other must manage to "turn around" each other to preserve their unity but at the same time advance towards their destination.

5   Experimental Results

5.1   Proxemic Distance Evaluation

We conducted several experiments with the above described model and simulator, to evaluate the plausibility of the overall system dynamics achieved with such simple basic rules and to calibrate the parameters to fit actual data available from the literature or acquired in the experiments. In particular, we first of all focused on the influence of the proxemic distance p on the overall system dynamics. We started considering Hall's personal distance as a starting point for this model parameter. Hall reported ranges for the various proxemic distances, considering a close phase and a far phase for all the different perceived distances (described in Section 3.1). In particular, we considered both an average value for the far phase of the personal distance (1m) and a low end value (75 cm) that is actually the border between the far and the close phases of the personal distance range. In general, the higher value allowed to achieve relatively results in scenarios characterized by a low density of pedestrians in the environment. For densities close and above one pedestrian per square meter, the lower value allowed achieving a smoother flow, more consistent with the results available in the literature.

A summary of the achieved results is shown in Fig. 4: the graphs represent the fundamental diagrams [36] of the data achieved in the simulation of a 10 m long and 5 m wide corridor. This kind of diagram shows how the average velocity of pedestrians

Fig. 3. Experiments on facing groups: several experiments were conducted on real pedestrian dynamics, some of which also considered the presence of groups of pedestrians, that were instructed on the fact that they had to behave as friends or relatives while moving during the experiment

varies according to the density of the simulated environment. Since the flow of pedestrians is directly proportional to their velocity, this diagram is sometimes presented in an equivalent form that shows the variation of flow according to the density. In general, we expect to have a decrease in the velocity when density grows; the flow, instead, initially grows, since it is also directly proportional to the density, until a certain threshold value is reached, then it decreases.

For these experiments we considered that the influence of the different components of pedestrian behaviour (i.e. the weights of their contribution to the overall movement vector), that is goal attraction, proxemic repulsion and group cohesion, is equal for the first two components while the third is less significant (about one third of the previous ones). This setting supported a good balance between flow smoothness, collision avoidance and group cohesion in a preliminary face validation phase.

We varied the number of agents altering the density of pedestrians in the environment; to keep constant the number of pedestrians in the corridor, the two ends were joined (i.e. pedestrians exiting from one end were actually re-entering the corridor from the other). For each run only complete pedestrian trips were considered (i.e. the first pedestrian exit event was discarded because related to a partial crossing of the corridor) and in high density scenarios a significant number of starting turns were also discarded to avoid transient starting conditions. The results of the simulations employing the low personal distance are consistent with empirical observations discussed in [36].

In parallel to the modeling effort, a set of experiments were conducted (in June 2010) to back-up with observed data some intuitions on the implications of the presence of groups in specific scenarios; two photos of one of the experiments are shown in Figure 3. In particular, this experiments is characterized by two sets of pedestrians moving in opposite directions in a constrained portion of space. In the set of pedestrians, in some of the experiments, some individuals were instructed to behave as friends or relatives, tying to stay close to each other in the movement towards their goal. It must be noted that this kind of situation is simple yet relevant for the understanding of some general principle on pedestrian movement and on the implications of the presence of groups in a

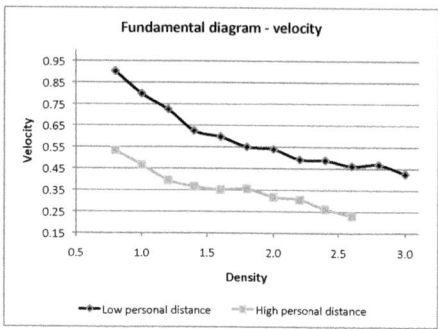 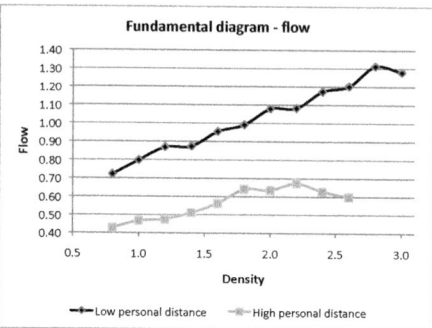

Fig. 4. Fundamental diagrams for the 10m long and 5m wide corridor scenario. The two data series respectively refer to different values for the proxemic distance, respectively the low end (75cm) and the average value (1m) of personal distance.

crowd. The analysis of a first set of experiments were not conclusive on the effects of the presence of groups in the two facing sets of pedestrians (in some experiments the overall travel time was lower when groups were present, in other occasion it was longer), but the simulation results achieved with a low personal distance were consistently more in tune with the observed data than those achieved with a high personal distance.

5.2   Groups and Individuals

We also analyzed the implications of the presence of groups in the environment. The data gathered in empirical observations still does not lead to conclusive results. However, simulation results are consistent with the available data and with other experiments carried out with a different model [5] characterized by similar behavioural rules but by a discrete spatial structure of the environment.

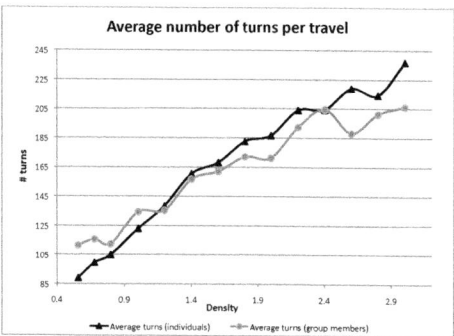 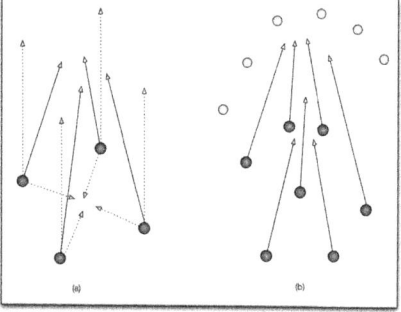

Fig. 5. On the left, a graph showing the average number of turns per travel, individuals compared to group members. On the right two different situations in which the front group member does not move at full speed (a) and in which following group members can easily advance due to the movement of front group members.

In simulations carried out in low density scenarios the average speed of group members is consistently lower than the one of single individuals. It must be considered that, when compared to basic individuals, their overall movement has an additional component that often diminishes the tendency to move towards the goal, in order to stay close to other group members. In high density scenarios, instead, the average speed of group members is generally higher than that of single individuals. This is generally due to the fact that the presence of the group has a greater influence on the possibility of other individuals to move, generating for instance a higher possibility of members on the back of the group to follow the "leaders". Figure 5 compares the average number of turns per complete travel time of individuals and group members in the same conditions of the experiments described in the previous section and it also depicts the above described situations of group dynamics.

6   Conclusions and Future Works

The paper has presented the research setting in which an innovative agent–based pedestrian an crowd modeling and simulation effort is set. Preliminary results of the first stage of the modeling phase were described. Future works are aimed, on one hand, at consolidating the preliminary results of this first scenarios, but also extending the range of simulated scenarios characterized by relatively simple spatial structures for the environment (e.g. bends, junctions). On the other hand, we want to better formalize the agent behavioural model and its overall architecture, but we also plan to extend the notion of group, in order to capture phenomenologies that are particularly relevant in the context of Hajj (e.g. hierarchical groups, but also hierarchies of groups). Finally, we are working at the integration of these models into an existing open source framework for 3D computing (Blender[4]), also to be able to embed these models and simulations in real portions of the built environment defined with traditional CAD tools.

Acknowledgments. This work is a result of the Crystal Project, funded by the Centre of Research Excellence in Hajj and Omrah (Hajjcore), Umm Al-Qura University, Makkah, Saudi Arabia.

References

1. Understanding crowd behaviours: Supporting evidence (2009),
   http://www.cabinetoffice.gov.uk/news/understanding-crowd
   -behaviours
2. Axtell, R.: Why Agents? On the Varied Motivations for Agent Computing in the Social Sciences. Center on Social and Economic Dynamics Working Paper 17 (2000)
3. Bandini, S., Federici, M.L., Vizzari, G.: Situated cellular agents approach to crowd modeling and simulation. Cybernetics and Systems 38(7), 729–753 (2007)
4. Bandini, S., Manenti, L., Manzoni, S., Sartori, F.: A knowledge-based approach to crowd classification. In: Proceedings of the 5th International Conference on Pedestrian and Evacuation Dynamics, March 8-10 (2010)

---

[4] http://www.blender.org/

5. Bandini, S., Rubagotti, F., Vizzari, G., Shimura, K.: An Agent Model of Pedestrian and Group Dynamics: Experiments on Group Cohesion. In: Pirrone, R., Sorbello, F. (eds.) AI*IA 2011. LNCS, vol. 6934, pp. 104–116. Springer, Heidelberg (2011)
6. Bandini, S., Manzoni, S., Redaelli, S.: Towards an Ontology for Crowds Description: A Proposal Based on Description Logic. In: Umeo, H., Morishita, S., Nishinari, K., Komatsuzaki, T., Bandini, S. (eds.) ACRI 2008. LNCS, vol. 5191, pp. 538–541. Springer, Heidelberg (2008)
7. Batty, M.: Agent based pedestrian modeling (editorial). Environment and Planning B: Planning and Design 28, 321–326 (2001)
8. Batty, M.: Agent-based pedestrian modelling. In: Advanced Spatial Analysis: The CASA Book of GIS, pp. 81–106. Esri Press (2003)
9. Blue, V.J., Adler, J.L.: Cellular automata microsimulation of bi-directional pedestrian flows. Transportation Research Record 1678, 135–141 (2000)
10. Blue, V.J., Adler, J.L.: Modeling four-directional pedestrian flows. Transportation Research Record 1710, 20–27 (2000)
11. Canetti, E.: Crowds and power. Farrar, Straus and Giroux (1984)
12. Chattaraj, U., Seyfried, A., Chakroborty, P.: Comparison of pedestrian fundamental diagram across cultures. Advances in Complex Systems 12(3), 393–405 (2009)
13. Christley, S., Zhu, X., Newman, S.A., Alber, M.S.: Multiscale agent-based simulation for chondrogenic pattern formation in vitro. Cybernetics and Systems 38(7), 707–727 (2007)
14. Dijkstra, J., Jessurun, J., de Vries, B., Timmermans, H.J.P.: Agent architecture for simulating pedestrians in the built environment. In: International Workshop on Agents in Traffic and Transportation, pp. 8–15 (2006)
15. Gloor, C., Stucki, P., Nagel, K.: Hybrid Techniques for Pedestrian Simulations. In: Sloot, P.M.A., Chopard, B., Hoekstra, A.G. (eds.) ACRI 2004. LNCS, vol. 3305, pp. 581–590. Springer, Heidelberg (2004)
16. Hall, E.T.: A system for the notation of proxemic behavior. American Anthropologist 65(5), 1003–1026 (1963), http://www.jstor.org/stable/668580
17. Hall, E.T.: The Hidden Dimension. Anchor Books (1966)
18. Helbing, D.: A fluid–dynamic model for the movement of pedestrians. Complex Systems 6(5), 391–415 (1992)
19. Helbing, D., Molnár, P.: Social force model for pedestrian dynamics. Phys. Rev. E 51(5), 4282–4286 (1995)
20. Helbing, D., Schweitzer, F., Keltsch, J., Molnár, P.: Active walker model for the formation of human and animal trail systems. Physical Review E 56(3), 2527–2539 (1997)
21. Henein, C.M., White, T.: Agent-Based Modelling of Forces in Crowds. In: Davidsson, P., Logan, B., Takadama, K. (eds.) MABS 2004. LNCS (LNAI), vol. 3415, pp. 173–184. Springer, Heidelberg (2005)
22. Kuligowski, E.D., Gwynne, S.M.V.: The Need for Behavioral Theory in Evacuation Modeling. In: Pedestrian and Evacuation Dynamics 2008, pp. 721–732. Springer, Heidelberg (2010)
23. Luck, M., McBurney, P., Sheory, O., Willmott, S. (eds.): Agent Technology: Computing as Interaction. University of Southampton (2005)
24. Moussaïd, M., Perozo, N., Garnier, S., Helbing, D., Theraulaz, G.: The walking behaviour of pedestrian social groups and its impact on crowd dynamics. PLoS ONE 5(4), e10047 (2010), http://dx.doi.org/10.1371%2Fjournal.pone.0010047
25. Murakami, Y., Ishida, T., Kawasoe, T., Hishiyama, R.: Scenario description for multi-agent simulation. In: AAMAS, pp. 369–376. ACM (2003)
26. Musse, S.R., Thalmann, D.: Hierarchical model for real time simulation of virtual human crowds. IEEE Trans. Vis. Comput. Graph. 7(2), 152–164 (2001)

27. Nagel, K., Schreckenberg, M.: A cellular automaton model for freeway traffic. Journal de Physique I France 2(2221), 222–235 (1992)

28. Nishinari, K., Suma, Y., Yanagisawa, D., Tomoeda, A., Kimura, A., Nishi, R.: Toward Smooth Movement of Crowds. In: Pedestrian and Evacuation Dynamics 2008, pp. 293–308. Springer, Heidelberg (2008)

29. Okazaki, S.: A study of pedestrian movement in architectural space, part 1: Pedestrian movement by the application of magnetic models. Transactions of A.I.J. (283), 111–119 (1979)

30. Paris, S., Donikian, S.: Activity-driven populace: A cognitive approach to crowd simulation. IEEE Computer Graphics and Applications 29(4), 34–43 (2009)

31. Pengfei, X., Lees, M., Nan, H., Viswanthatn, T.V.: Validation of Agent-Based Simulation through Human Computation: An Example of Crowd Simulation. In: Villatoro, D., Sabater-Mir, J., Sichman, J.S. (eds.) MABS 2011. LNCS (LNAI), vol. 7124, pp. 90–102. Springer, Heidelberg (2011)

32. Qiu, F., Hu, X.: Modeling group structures in pedestrian crowd simulation. Simulation Modelling Practice and Theory 18(2), 190–205 (2010)

33. Reynolds, C.W.: Flocks, herds and schools: A distributed behavioral model. In: SIGGRAPH 1987: Proceedings of the 14th Annual Conference on Computer Graphics and Interactive Techniques, pp. 25–34. ACM, New York (1987)

34. Sarmady, S., Haron, F., Talib, A.Z.H.: Modeling groups of pedestrians in least effort crowd movements using cellular automata. In: Al-Dabass, D., Triweko, R., Susanto, S., Abraham, A. (eds.) Asia International Conference on Modelling and Simulation, pp. 520–525. IEEE Computer Society (2009)

35. Schadschneider, A., Kirchner, A., Nishinari, K.: Ca Approach to Collective Phenomena in Pedestrian Dynamics. In: Bandini, S., Chopard, B., Tomassini, M. (eds.) ACRI 2002. LNCS, vol. 2493, pp. 239–248. Springer, Heidelberg (2002)

36. Schadschneider, A., Klingsch, W., Klüpfel, H., Kretz, T., Rogsch, C., Seyfried, A.: Evacuation dynamics: Empirical results, modeling and applications. In: Meyers, R.A. (ed.) Encyclopedia of Complexity and Systems Science, pp. 3142–3176. Springer, Heidelberg (2009)

37. Schreckenberg, M., Sharma, S.D. (eds.): Pedestrian and Evacuation Dynamics. Springer, Heidelberg (2001)

38. Shao, W., Terzopoulos, D.: Autonomous pedestrians. Graphical Models 69(5-6), 246–274 (2007)

39. Toyama, M.C., Bazzan, A.L.C., da Silva, R.: An agent-based simulation of pedestrian dynamics: from lane formation to auditorium evacuation. In: Nakashima, H., Wellman, M.P., Weiss, G., Stone, P. (eds.) 5th International Joint Conference on Autonomous Agents and Multiagent Systems (AAMAS 2006), pp. 108–110. ACM Press (2006)

40. Wąs, J.: Crowd Dynamics Modeling in the Light of Proxemic Theories. In: Rutkowski, L., Scherer, R., Tadeusiewicz, R., Zadeh, L.A., Zurada, J.M. (eds.) ICAISC 2010, Part II. LNCS, vol. 6114, pp. 683–688. Springer, Heidelberg (2010)

41. Willis, A., Gjersoe, N., Havard, C., Kerridge, J., Kukla, R.: Human movement behaviour in urban spaces: Implications for the design and modelling of effective pedestrian environments. Environment and Planning B 31(6), 805–828 (2004)

42. Xu, S., Duh, H.B.L.: A simulation of bonding effects and their impacts on pedestrian dynamics. IEEE Transactions on Intelligent Transportation Systems 11(1), 153–161 (2010)

Validation of Agent-Based Simulation through Human Computation: An Example of Crowd Simulation

Pengfei Xing, Michael Lees*, Hu Nan, and T. Vaisagh Viswanthatn

School of Computer Engineering,
Nanyang Technological University,
Singapore, 639798
{pfxing,mhlees}@ntu.edu.sg, {huna0002,vaisagh1}@e.ntu.edu.sg

Abstract. Agent-based modeling as a methodology for understanding natural phenomena is becoming increasingly popular in many disciplines of scientific research. Validation is still a significant problem for agent-based modelers and while various validation methodologies have been proposed, none have been widely adopted. Data plays a key role in the validation of any simulation system, typically large amounts of observable real world data are necessary to compare with model outputs. However, the complex nature of the studied natural systems will often make data collection difficult. This is certainly true for crowd and egress simulation, where data is limited and difficult to collect. In this paper we propose a new technique for validation of agent-based models, particularly those which relate to human behavior. This methodology adopts ideas from the field of Human Computation as a means of collecting large amounts of contextual behavioral data. The key principle is to use games as a means of framing behavioral questions to try and capture people's natural and instinctive decisions. We outline some key design challenges for such games and present one example game in the form of Escape. Escape is an egress based game where people are tasked to escape from rooms inhabited by other people. We show some preliminary studies which highlight some interesting applications of the game in addressing validation of behavioral based crowd and egress simulation.

Keywords: Simulation, Validation, Games, Human Computation.

1 Introduction

The term Complex System [9] has been used to describe systems, which are a formation of interconnected components that exhibit emergent complex behavior. The field of Agent-Based Modeling and Simulation (ABMS) is a popular field of modeling and simulation that is ideally suited to simulate such systems. An agent-based model is defined by a collection of interacting autonomous agents

---

* Corresponding author.

D. Villatoro, J. Sabater-Mir, and J.S. Sichman (Eds.): MABS 2011, LNAI 7124, pp. 90–102, 2012.

with individually defined properties and behaviors. Through development of simple rules and the complex temporal interactions of the many agents, more complex macro level system properties will emerge. From a modeling perspective this is an attractive method for reasoning about complex systems since many forms of complex system the individual behaviors and characteristics are well understood, or easy to describe. Given this understanding it is clear to see why ABMS has seen a dramatic increase in its application in a wide variety of disciplines including: Sociology, Biology, and Economics. However, the major motivation for using ABMS to understand complex systems has an undesirable consequence when ascertaining the validity of models. One central motivation for ABMS is that the behavior of the system emerges in some unknown and unexpected way. This unpredictable nature of the system makes agent-based models very challenging to validate and current approaches and techniques are still under-developed with many philosophical and methodical questions remaining unanswered [14].

Validation is important for simulation; without some form of validation and verification there can only be limited confidence in the accuracy of the model. As explained, agent-based models pose unique challenges with regard to validation and these challenges become even more significant when trying to model natural systems which involve human behavioral aspects, such as crowd or egress simulation. For these types of model, challenges occur in many aspects of validation: collection of appropriate data, the non-determinism of human free will, etc. Establishing hard validation for such systems is very difficult [10,14]; it is perhaps better to state that one gains confidence in the simulation by experimentation and comparison with observable data. Despite these problems associated with validity, simulations which consider human behavior still have their place, and are widely applied in areas of critical importance (e.g., epidemics [4], finance [12]). Due to the stochastic nature of these systems, both simulation replication and an abundance of related data are critical. Through repetition, results will have an associated confidence, which can help modellers understand the likelihood of the obtained result.

It is possible to achieve validation in a number of ways, and the suitability of approaches is often dependent on the motivation of modelling [3,17]. Epstein [3] pointed out that the goal for models is not always prediction, but rather explanation. Epstein believes that in social science, models can be used to help guide data collection. In this way models can be meaningful in illuminating core dynamics. However, for ensuring predictive power, validation and data are important; modellers must be able to show that their model is capable of producing some known output data for a given set of known input data. Without this validation process it is hard to make any claims about the predictive power of a model. As well as validation, the data available from a physical system affects the experimental frame, the model resolution and model instantiation. This is what makes egress or crowd simulation so hard to validate and justify; data for emergency evacuation scenarios is very limited. The data that is available, is often at an aggregate level, e.g., number of people through exit, density of people, etc. More sophisticated techniques, such as video tracking, are still limited in terms of accuracy and throughput of data collection. The use of engineered experiments also has significant limitations, recreating the stressful conditions of a real evacuation is very difficult under controlled conditions. Safety constrains the experimental conditions such that participants must be given prior knowledge of the conditions and therefore will not feel the same pressure or fear. Another key challenge is the non-deterministic nature of people's behavior during egress. Therefore, to obtain confidence in the data, and hence validation, one must obtain multiple instances of the same data sets. Again, the difficulty of obtaining such data makes this validation an exigent task.

In this paper we propose a novel method for validation of agent-based evacuation and crowd simulation using concepts from the field of Human Computation [21]. We introduce our iPhone/iPad evacuation game which is intended to procure data and information, which can then be utilized in agent-based crowd and evacuation simulations we are currently developing [11]. The game is still in the early stages of development and as such the data collected is intended to be illustrative. The key contribution of this paper is therefore to introduce the concept of validation through human computation and to illustrate the usefulness and feasibility of such an approach. The remainder of this paper is organized as follows, section two introduces the simulation application area of crowd simulation and discusses what type of data is necessary for different simulation approaches and how it can be applied. Section three summarizes the field of Human Computation and provides a survey of significant and related work in the area. Section four continues with a detailed description of the evacuation game and its design. Section five outlines the three test cases used in this paper and presents some initial findings and the implications for crowd simulation models. The paper concludes with a summary and some possible directions for future work.

2   Related Work

Human crowds and their egress can and have been modelled in a number of ways; existing systems apply techniques such as flow modeling , particle systems, cellular automata and agent-based behavioral models. Each modeling approach has its own benefits along with its own drawbacks. A flow-based approach [19] works well under certain conditions where a homogeneous, optimal behavior is appropriate. This is typically in very high density locations where individual choice has little impact on the overall crowd motion or egress. The force-based particle systems [8] assume individuals (or particles) in the crowd exert forces on each other. Motion of individuals is then calculated by resolving the interacting forces on each individual agent. This approach allows for greater heterogeneity in the crowd, but interactions between individual must be described in terms of opposing forces, which can make it hard to quantify complex interactions and decisions. Cellular automata models [24] offer a great deal of heterogeneity, for example models for exit choice can consider exit size and exit density [5]. Many models focus on the physical aspects of crowd motion, such as density, exit throughput and congestion. While these issues are clearly essential when analyzing egress or crowd motion, there are other, non-physical factors, which can greatly affect egress effectiveness. In [11] a cognitive agent framework was developed to provide tools for modeling human crowds. This framework incorporated many non-physical issues, for example: emotion, group formation, and gender and age variation. Other existing egress and crowd models have considered different cognitive aspects, in particular socials norm [15], panic [15] and emotion [11]. While the arguments for this naturalistic approach seem convincing, the real challenge comes about in validating the approach and verifying its implementation.

Validation is typically application specific, every natural system will present unique challenges for validation. The ABMS community has identified specific issues associated with validating agent-based models. Some have correctly argued the need for a systematic approach and methodology for validating the models which are developed [10]. Others have discussed traditional (empirical) and alternative notions of validity and their implications in the context of agent-based modeling [14,25]. From the perspective of behavioral simulation some have suggested expert based facial validation as one feasible approach [6]. This popular approach involves generating observable output from the simulation and asking a domain expert to assess the likelihood of the derived output from the given input. Sterman [18] proposed direct experimental validation as the most appropriate way to validate behavioral simulations. His arguments and approach closely mirror those which we propose in this paper. Sterman designed contextual games and scenarios in which to place subjects. These real life "role-play" scenarios, or interactive surveys, would be used to verify and test rules proposed within the simulation. The game would be controlled to present the subject with the precise scenarios in which the rules are intended to apply. The response can then be compared with the contextual rules, as specified in the model. While we agree with this approach to validating behavior based models, the approach does not scale well when the model requires the response of many participants. One of the distinct advantages which the human computation approach affords the experimenter, is the ability to conduct large scale interactive surveys. Having a ubiquitous game also allows data to be collected from many different countries with vastly different cultural and social behavior.

From the perspective of egress or crowd simulation there have been a number of attempts to validate various types of models. Statistical validation approaches generally look at macroscopic or aggregate properties of the real crowd and try to recreate the same properties within the model [1]. Obtaining data from a real crowd is also difficult, this can be achieved through manual counting, simple mechanical counting or through the use of video analysis [2]. Such approaches are valuable, but validation is still very context dependent and a model with various individual characteristics would need some way of knowing the approximate initial crowd composition in order to guarantee the model and system correspond. Facial validation is also one popular approach for validating virtual crowds, [16] uses a form of interactive survey whereby participants were placed in a virtual world and surrounded by a computer generated crowd. Participants were then questioned about their experience and in particular their impressions of the artificial crowd.

3 Human Computation

Human computation is a method for utilizing humans as computational elements. In much the same way as other distributed computing platforms utilize idle clock cycles of a CPU (e.g., BOINC), human computation attempts to utilize idle human cycles through games. Typically the games will be carefully designed in order to make a repetitive mundane task interesting, which in turn will encourage people to play the game and unknowingly perform the task. Many researchers have collected fascinating statistics as to the number of man-hours spent on gaming around the world. As one example Jane McGonigal [13] has suggested the average American 21 year old will have spent 10000 hours of their lives playing games, which is approximately the same number of hours that same person will have spent within the education system. On May 23rd 2010 the Google main page was changed to include a version of the classic PacMan game, some estimations are that 4.82 million man hours of productivity were lost in a single day (approximately US$120 million). The core motivation of Human Computation is to attempt to exploit this resource by designing games with some productive or positive side-effect.

As well as the massive amount of computational resources offered, humans are also capable of types of computation which machines cannot perform. One example of this is the ability to assign meaning to images through meta tagging, see (ESP Game and Peek-a-boom [22,23]). The principle can be further refined to state that humans can be used to generate data by playing games, which can then be used by machines. In the ESP game for example, players are asked to textually identify contents of images and will succeed once they match the same word with their playing partner (who is randomly assigned via the internet based game). This way the humans, by playing the game, are generating image meta data (i.e., stating an image contains a car, house, grass, etc.) which can then be used by Google image search (or similar search engine). Current machine vision techniques are not capable of assigning such semantics to image contents, and so the alternative to such games would be to ask thousands of people to manually describe the contents of the billions of images on the internet. In this paper we adapt this concept to the validation of beahvioral models, that is we propose developing games which will be used to collect instictive beahvioral responses, which can then be used to quantitatively validate behavioral models.

4 The Game: Escape

When designing games with a specific purpose, as is the case with human computation, there are a number of important considerations which must be accounted for [20]. From the perspective of simulation validation, there are further unique design criteria which must be incorporated in the game design. During the design process we have considered the following principles:

1. *Accuracy*: The game mechanics and artificially controlled players need to be designed carefully so as to closely reflect reality. We don't claim or strive for completely correct behavior for the artificial crowd in the game. What is important is that the player perceives the artificial crowd as human-like and therefore, makes the same decision in the game as they would in the equivalent real world scenario.
2. *Experimental Control*: In order to be able to draw conclusions from each of the scenarios, it is important that the experimenter is able to easily control conditions. If the experimenter wants to study the effects of one particular control on the players decision, the levels should be designed carefully to factor out as many other possible variables which may affect decisions.
3. *Ubiquity*: One fundamental benefit of the human computation approach for validation is the ability to collect large amounts of data. Therefore it is critical that the game receives the correct level of exposure and is played by as many people as possible.
4. *Playability*: Obviously it is important that the game is enjoyable to play so players will continue to play the game. This principle in fact contains all the standard game design fundamentals which have been developed over the past four decades of computer game development.

None of the above are trivial tasks and the development of a successful computer game is typically a slow and iterative process. The current incarnation of Escape has attempted to address the first three design principles of accuracy, experimental control and pervasiveness. The experiments conducted for this paper attempt to somewhat verify the accuracy of the game mechanics. It is important to note that the above principles will often lead to conflicting requirements for the game, which necessitate a number of trade-offs. For example, The choice of the iPhone as the platform was mainly for reasons of exposure and the ubiquity of the system. We decided against a more immersive, powerful 3D platform as this would be both harder to develop and would have lesser exposure, which in turn would result in fewer samples.

Our game, *Escape*, has been developed as an iPhone application using an open source game engine Cocos2D-iPhone. The game is still in the developmental stage and while all the game mechanics and level designer have been fully developed, the game still lacks a polished graphical front-end and storyline. We currently have two separate applications available: the Escape game itself and a convenient level editor for experimenters to quickly develop new scenarios with specific objectives in mind. The game itself consists of a single human agent controlled by the player and some number of competing AI controlled agents. Obstacles and walls are configured, as well as specific target locations which trigger level completion. In the level editor, level designers can simply click, drag and drop to design the shapes and positions of obstacles and goals (and sub-goals) and positions of agents.

The level designer is used in four distinct stages, firstly obstacles are drawn as a polygon from a set of user specified points. The designer must then specify a series of roadmaps, which are necessary for the RVO2 [7] motion planning system we adopt. In the third stage the designer specifies the AI controlled agents initial location and desired goals, and in the final stage the player agent is specified along with its goal. Once complete, the level specification is output to an XML file which can be loaded into the game or loaded back into the level editor if modification is required.

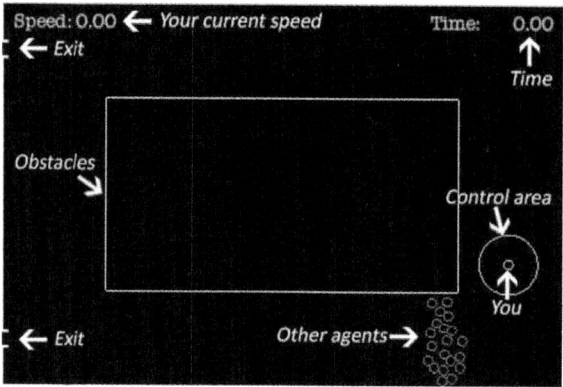

Fig. 1. The Escape game

The game itself (see Figure 1) is essentially a time-stepped simulation where the AI agents are performing sense-think-act cycles within each time step. Obviously the hardware on even modern iPhones is somewhat limited, so the time step must be chosen appropriately to achieve the correct level of interactivity and playability - this is currently set to be 0.25 seconds. The AI controlled agents use the RVO2 motion planning system which has previously been applied to crowd simulation. The agents are $0.4m$ in diameter and have a series of specified waypoints, a preferred velocity for each agent is calculated using the current location of the AI agent and its current sub-goal. This preferred velocity is passed into the RVO2 calculation and an actual velocity is calculated, which will try to avoid any oncoming collisions with minimal deviation from the specified preferred velocity. The human player controls the player agent by drawing (i.e., dragging with a finger) a preferred velocity, the actual motion of the player agent is also governed by the RVO2 mechanism[1]. Once a level is completed and the user agent escapes, a file is written to the phone which records the positions of all agents at every time step during that level. These files are then processed and analysed to obtain the desired results from the game.

---

[1] In theory any motion planning system could be employed within the game, we chose RVO2 in particular as it produces high quality motion with high computational efficiency.

5 Test Scenarios

In this paper we present preliminary results from two test scenarios we feel arc important for validating behavioral crowd simulation models. These tests have been conducted on a relatively small scale, with 25 participants. This preliminary study is intended to achieve a number of different objectives. Firstly, the results will offer an initial insight into the behavior of people in the chosen scenarios. Secondly, they should highlight any issues with the current game mechanics and allow the game to be improved prior to general release. Finally, the initial tests should enable refinement of the scenarios and test cases to ensure we are measuring the correct behavioral decisions.

Each participant is asked to play a total of 12 different level instances (6 of each type) with varying environmental configurations. The sample set are predominantly members of Parallel and Distributed Computing Centre (PDCC) within the school of Computer Engineering. Other participants have been sourced through word of mouth. All tests are conducted on an iPad running IOS 4.2.1. The game begins with an information entry screen where a participant is asked to enter their name, gender, age and place of birth. This information is stored within each output file generated during the game. Once the participant has entered their details, they are presented with a short game description outlining the purpose of the game and their objectives.

5.1 Density and Distance

One behavior which is common to many egress models is the trade-off made by people when opting for less crowded but longer routes. Obviously this trade-off is different for different people and any correct behavioral model should account for this, the difficulty is in understanding the average tradeoff made by an average person, or by a specific type of person. The scenario used here presents the player with two route choices R_1 and R_2 (See Figure 2(a))the experimenter can vary the relative distance and density of both routes, thereby obtaining the average behavior of a number of players for a given configuration.

Figure 2(a) shows the environmental configuration for this experiment. The player is presented with two exit choices involving a longer route (R_1) and a shorter route (R_2). Six different initial conditions of this scenario are presented to the player during the experiments. The number of agents occupying space on route R_2 is varied from zero to fifty in increments of ten. The computer controlled agents will always choose exit E_2 and are created within the area A (See Figure 2(a)). Given the initial configuration (and a fixed random seed) for each scenario it would be possible to calculate the optimal route choice in terms of escape time. However, one of the critical aspects of this experiment is that humans do not necessarily make optimal decisions in such scenarios, our experiments will hopefully offer some insight into exactly when and why humans choose the non-optimal route.

Figure 2(b) presents the summarized results from this test case. The results indicate even with a relatively small sample size we are achieving a definite transition in behavior. Once the route R_2 is occupied with more than 10 agents the majority of people will opt for the longer, but empty route R_1. Further experiments could clarify the exact point at which the likelihood of choosing either of the two routes becomes the same. It would also be interesting to understand how the choice varies with a greater distinction in route length.

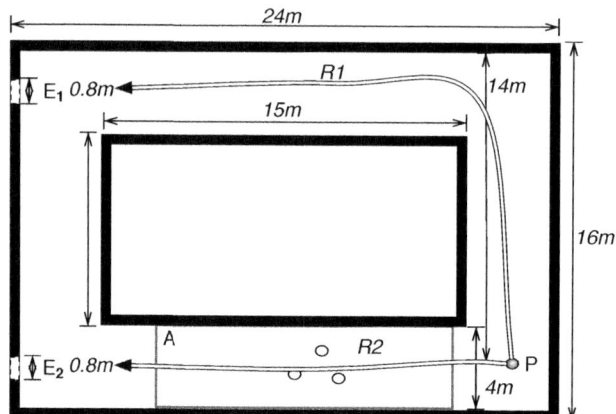

(a) The Density vs. Distance Scenario Configuration.

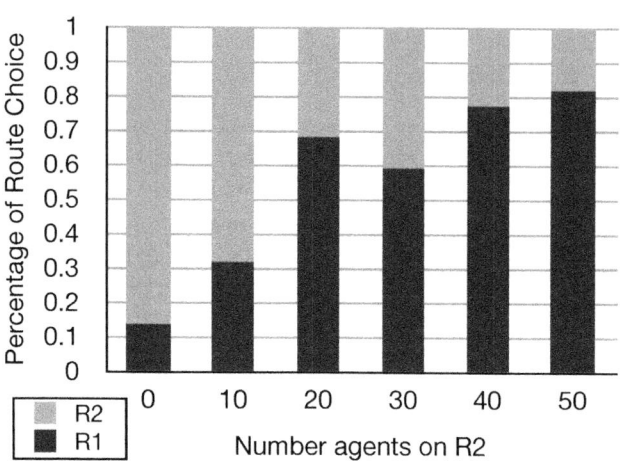

(b) Percentage of participants selecting routes R_1 and R_2 for different numbers of agents on R_2.

Fig. 2. Density and Distance Scenario

5.2   Exit Size

The second case study examines the effect that exit size has when an evacuee chooses their exit. The literature contains many examples of behavioral rules which use exit size, exit throughput and exit density (e.g., [5]). However, the assumption that a human can quickly and accurately calculate exit throughput and density is perhaps incorrect. This game scenario is intended to investigate the hypothesis that in fact exit size alone can be the determining factor when making an exit choice.

Figure 3(a) depicts the environment used in this case study, the player is placed in the centre of the room with two exits at equal distance. The environment is populated with 50 other AI controlled agents placed uniformly in the circular area indicated by A in Figure 3(a). The AI agents will attempt to leave the environment through either of the two exits. There are again six different instances of this case study (presented as six different levels), with the relative number of agents choosing each exit varying in each instance. The larger exit is chosen to be twice the size of the smaller exit and the probability of an AI agent choosing the small exit (E_1) varied between $0, 0.2, 0.4, 0.6, 0.8$ and 1.0.

Figure 3(b) presents the summarized results from this test case. As expected, it seems that in most cases the participants will opt for the larger of the two exits regardless of the relative proportion of AI agents choosing the small exit. However, a slight increase in those players choosing E_2 can be observed as the number of AI agents choosing E_2 decreases. For the case when all agents choose exit E_1 the results show a surprising change in behavior. From experimental observation we realize this is due to the level specification. In this case the player is pushed toward the smaller exit by the other agents who are all moving to E_1. The player typically attempts to move towards the larger exit, but due to pushing, eventually submits to the will of the crowd and chooses the smaller exit. This result emphasizes the need for careful scenario testing to ensure they are correctly designed to present a valid set of choices to the player.

6   Discussion and Future Work

In this paper we have proposed a new approach to validating agent-based models which uses principles from the field of Human Computation. This approach is well suited to validating human behavior models which are known to present unique challenges in terms of validation. We do not see this methodology as a single technique for achieving validation for all forms of agent-based models or behavioral models. Instead we view it as a complementary approach to existing methods and another technique modelers can utilize when building confidence in their models. Importantly, our technique has the key advantage of being able to generate large sets of data from a large sample set. The approach also offers the advantages outlined by Sterman [18], in that using carefully designed scenarios and games provides a more contextual and interactive form for phrasing the question. This paper also presented the game Escape as an example of using human computation as a way to validate behavioral crowd simulation. Our assumption is that the simple 2D interface is capable of capturing the same reactive decisions that people make in reality. This may be a strong assumption and is something which we plan to investigate in future work. One can argue that this is equivalent to other forms of facial validation where experts are asked to

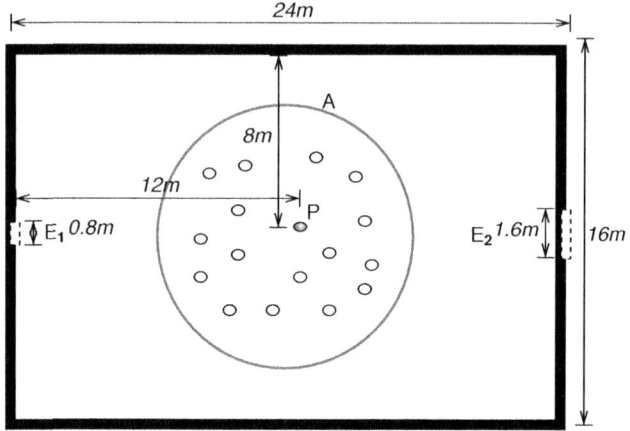

(a) Exit Size Scenario Configuration.

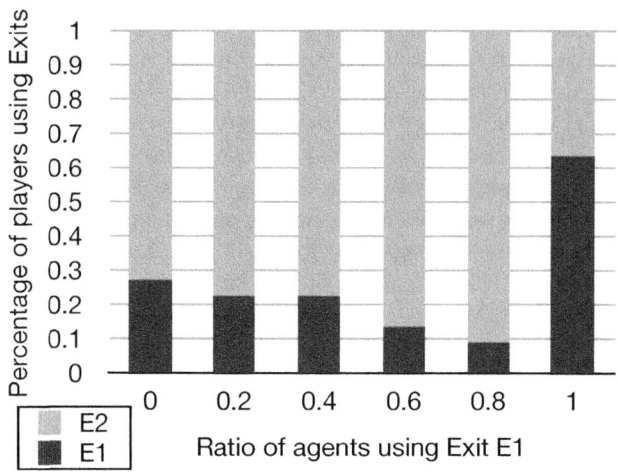

(b) Percentage of participants selecting exit E_1 and E_2 for different ratio of AI agents using E_1.

Fig. 3. Exit Size Scenario

observe 2D animation output from the crowd simualtion. Initial results indicate the feasibility of the approach, but also highlight the challenges in designing appropriate scenarios. We believe that eventually the resultant focused and statistical data can be applied in the development, parameterization and validation of decision models and route algorithms for crowd simulation.

There are still a number of issues we hope to address in our continued work. Firstly, Escape will be completed and a game story will be constructed around the current basic game mechanics. Once the graphics and story have been completed, we plan for further testing before placing the game on general release. We still have to clarify issues of data collection from phones prior to release and methods for distributing new game levels and scenarios. Game controls may also be developed to allow for other scenario types. For example, in all current scenarios the player has complete information regarding the environment, we plan to develop scenarios with limited sensor range to test other possible decision cases. One important question is the accuracy of the game and the correctness of the behavioral data that is collected. It is important that the game itself is validated against real world data. We are currently looking at the use of video or RFID tracking with real world experiments as two possible methods for validating Escape. In this paper we have presented a method for collecting data which can in principle be used for validation purposes, we have not shown the entire procedure and actually validated an exisitng model. This is, we feel, beyond the scope of a single paper. However, in future work we plan to functionally validate a group-based perception model we are developing.

Acknowledgments. This research has been funded by the NTU SU Grant M58020019.

References

1. Banerjee, B., Kraemer, L.: Validation of agent based crowd egress simulation. In: Proceedings of the 9th International Conference on Autonomous Agents and Multiagent Systems, AAMAS 2010, vol. 1, pp. 1551–1552. International Foundation for Autonomous Agents and Multiagent Systems, Richland (2010)
2. Berrou, J., Beecham, J., Quaglia, P., Kagarlis, M., Gerodimos, A.: Calibration and validation of the legion simulation model using empirical data. In: Waldau, N., Gattermann, P., Knoflacher, H., Schreckenberg, M. (eds.) Pedestrian and Evacuation Dynamics 2005, pp. 167–181. Springer, Heidelberg (2007)
3. Epstein, J.M.: Why model? Journal of Artificial Societies and Social Simulation 11(4), 12 (2008)
4. Ferguson, N.M., Cummings, D.A.T., Fraser, C., Cajka, J.C., Cooley, P.C., Burke, D.S.: Strategies for mitigating an influenza pandemic. Nature 442(7101), 448–452 (2006)
5. Ferscha, A., Zia, K.: On the efficiency of lifebelt based crowd evacuation. In: Proceedings of the 2009 13th IEEE/ACM International Symposium on Distributed Simulation and Real Time Applications, DS-RT 2009, pp. 13–20. IEEE Computer Society, Washington, DC (2009)
6. Gonzalez, A.J.: Validation of human behavioral models. In: Proceedings of the Twelfth International Florida Artificial Intelligence Research Society Conference, pp. 489–493. AAAI Press (1999)
7. Guy, S.J., Chhugani, J., Curtis, S., Dubey, P., Lin, M., Manocha, D.: Pledestrians: a least-effort approach to crowd simulation. In: Proceedings of the 2010 ACM SIGGRAPH/Eurographics Symposium on Computer Animation, SCA 2010, pp. 119–128. Eurographics Association, Aire-la-Ville (2010)
8. Helbing, D., Molnár, P.: Social force model for pedestrian dynamics. Physical Review E 51(5), 4282–4286 (1995)
9. Jennings, N.R.: An agent-based approach for building complex software systems. Commun. ACM 44, 35–41 (2001)

10. Klügl, F.: A validation methodology for agent-based simulations. In: Proceedings of the, ACM Symposium on Applied Computing, SAC 2008, pp. 39–43. ACM, New York (2008)
11. Luo, L., Zhou, S., Cai, W., Low, M.Y.-H., Lees, M.: Toward a generic framework for modeling human behaviors in crowd simulation. In: IAT, pp. 275–278. IEEE (2009)
12. Lux, T., Marchesi, M.: Scaling and criticality in a stochastic multi-agent model of a financial market. Nature 397(6719), 498–500 (1999)
13. McGonical, J.: Gaming can make a better world. TED (February 2010), http://www.ted.com/talks/jane_mcgonigal_gaming_can_make_a_better_world.html
14. Moss, S.: Alternative approaches to the empirical validation of agent-based models. Journal of Artificial Societies and Social Simulation 11(1), 5 (2008)
15. Pan, X., Han, C., Dauber, K., Law, K.: A multi-agent based framework for the simulation of human and social behaviors during emergency evacuations. AI & Society 22, 113–132 (2007), doi:10.1007/s00146-007-0126-1
16. Pelechano, N., Stocker, C., Allbeck, J.M., Badler, N.I.: Being a part of the crowd: towards validating vr crowds using presence. In: AAMAS 2008 (1), pp. 136–142 (2008)
17. Sloot, P., Coveney, P., Dongarra, J.: Editorial board. Journal of Computational Science 1(4), CO2–CO2 (2010)
18. Sterman, J.: Testing behavioral simulation models by direct experiment. Working papers 1752-86. Massachusetts Institute of Technology (MIT), Sloan School of Management (1986)
19. Treuille, A., Cooper, S., Popović, Z.: Continuum crowds. In: SIGGRAPH 2006: ACM SIGGRAPH 2006 Papers, pp. 1160–1168. ACM, New York (2006)
20. von Ahn, L.: Games with a purpose. Computer 39, 92–94 (2006)
21. von Ahn, L.: Human computation. In: Proceedings of the 4th International Conference on Knowledge Capture, K-CAP 2007, pp. 5–6. ACM, New York (2007)
22. von Ahn, L., Dabbish, L.: Labeling images with a computer game. In: Proceedings of the SIGCHI Conference on Human Factors in Computing Systems, CHI 2004, pp. 319–326. ACM, New York (2004)
23. von Ahn, L., Liu, R., Blum, M.: Peekaboom: a game for locating objects in images. In: Proceedings of the SIGCHI Conference on Human Factors in Computing Systems, CHI 2006, pp. 55–64. ACM, New York (2006)
24. Weifeng, Y., Hai, T.K.: A novel algorithm of simulating multi-velocity evacuation based on cellular automata modeling and tenability condition. Physica A: Statistical Mechanics and its Applications 379(1), 250–262 (2007)
25. Windrum, P., Fagiolo, G., Moneta, A.: Empirical validation of agent-based models: Alternatives and prospects. Journal of Artificial Societies and Social Simulation 10(2), 8 (2007)

Observation of Large-Scale Multi-Agent Based Simulations

Gildas Morvan[1,2], Alexandre Veremme[1,3], and Daniel Dupont[1,3]

[1] Univ. Lille Nord de France, 1bis rue Georges Lefévre 59044 Lille cedex, France
[2] LGI2A, U. Artois, Technoparc Futura 62400 Béthune, France
`firstname.surname@univ-artois.fr`
[3] HEI, 13 rue de Toul 59046 Lille Cedex, France
`firstname.surname@hei.fr`

Abstract. The computational cost of large-scale multi-agent based simulations (MABS) can be extremely important, especially if simulations have to be monitored for validation purposes. In this paper, two methods, based on self-observation and statistical survey theory, are introduced in order to optimize the computation of observations in MABS. An empirical comparison of the computational cost of these methods is performed on a toy problem.

Keywords: large-scale multi-agent based simulations, observation methods, scalability.

1 Introduction

Theoretical and practical advances in the field of multi-agent based simulations (MABS) allow modelers to simulate very complex systems to solve real world problems. However the analysis and validation of simulations remain engineering problems that do not have "turnkey" solutions. Thus, MABS users conducting such tasks face two main issues:

1. define validation metrics for the simulation,
2. compute efficiently the metrics.

The first issue is generally solved by constructing a set of *ad-hoc* qualitative or quantitative rules on simulation properties. To evaluate these rules, it is then mandatory to observe the corresponding simulation properties and thus to consider the second issue. A distinctive characteristic of MABS is that global simulation properties are not necessary directly observable: they may need to be computed from local agent properties. Fortunately, most of modern MABS platforms come with observation frameworks and toolboxes. Basically, three types of observation methods are generally available [10]:

1. interactive observation: users select observed properties during simulations, *e.g.*, using a point and click interface,

D. Villatoro, J. Sabater-Mir, and J.S. Sichman (Eds.): MABS 2011, LNAI 7124, pp. 103–112, 2012.

2. brute-force direct observation: simulation agents sharing a given property are monitored; agent properties are then aggregated by a so-called *observer* agent that computes the observation (fig. 1),
3. indirect observation: the observed property is inferred from the observable consequences of agent actions, *e.g.*, in the environment.

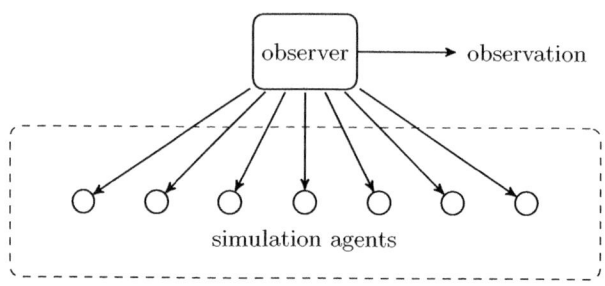

Fig. 1. Brute-force direct observation method

While the first method is clearly unadapted to the observation of large-scale or batch simulations, the second has an important computational cost. This issue is illustrated with a simple case study inspired by "StupidModel" [9]: N agents move randomly in a two dimensional environment $\mathcal{E}$ discretized into $100 \cdot 100$ square cells with Moore neighbourhood during 1000 steps. An area $\mathcal{Z} \subseteq \mathcal{E}$ is defined. The number of agents Z in the area $\mathcal{Z}$ is observed at each simulation step. This simulation is implemented on the MadKit/TurtleKit platform[1] [7]. Figure 2 shows the CPU times needed to compute unobserved and observed simulations on a Dell Precision 650 workstation[2], using indirect and brute-force direct observation methods, for the given expected value $E(Z) = N/5$, as a function of the number of simulation agents N.

This work is based on existing implementations (by MadKit/TurtleKit and MASON) of the direct observation method. Thus, an empirical computational complexity metric, *i.e.*, the CPU time needed to compute simulations, is used. This metric, denoted $\mathcal{C}$, depends, in our case study, on the number of simulation agents, N, and on the expected value of the cardinal of the subset of simulation agents computed by *filter*, $E(Z)$.

These results show that, in this case, indirect observation has a minor impact on the computational cost of the simulations. Kaminka *et al.* also note that this method is not intrusive: simulation agents do not have to be modified or accessed during the observation process [5]. However, Wilkins *et al.* underline that the applicability of this method is limited: the observed property might not

---

[1] All the simulations and observation methods described in this paper have also been implemented on the MASON platform [6], leading to similar results.

[2] CPU: 2×3.06 GHz Intel Xeon[TM], RAM: 4×1 GB. Full specification: http://www.dell.com/downloads/emea/products/precn/precn_650_uk.pdf. All the results presented in this paper have been computed by this machine.

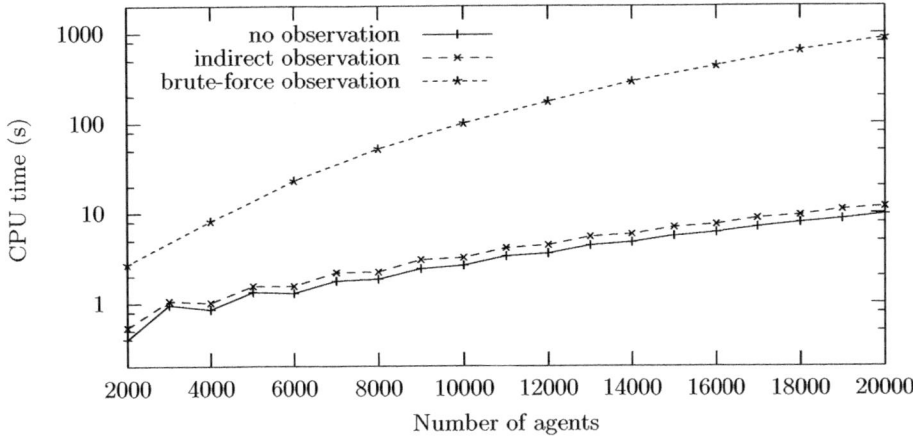

Fig. 2. CPU times (log scale) needed to compute observed and unobserved simulations for $E(Z) = N/5$

be inferred [13]; it is often true in complex, *i.e.*, in most of the real world, cases. Thus, direct observation often remains the only available option.

The brute-force direct observation method is, for this particular and very simple toy-problem, linear in the number of simulation agents[3], *i.e.*, $\mathcal{C}(obs) \propto N$, while the model is exponential, *i.e.*, $\mathcal{C}(model) \propto \alpha^N, \alpha > 1$. However, complex simulations generally involve non-linear observation problems [12]. Thus, improving direct observation appears to be a good lead to improve the efficiency of large-scale complex MABS.

In this paper, two non-brute-force direct observation methods, based on self-observation and statistical survey theory are introduced. An empirical comparison of the computational cost of these methods is performed and discussed on the presented case study.

2   Filtrated Direct Observation of MABS

Basically, there are two ways to compute a direct observation:

1. a set of agents $\mathcal{A}$ (generally all the simulation agents that share the properties that have to be observed), statically defined, is probed by an observer agent,
2. a subset $\mathcal{A}'$ of $\mathcal{A}$, computed at runtime, is probed (fig. 3).

Formally, we consider an observation function

$$obs : 2^{\mathcal{A}} \to \mathcal{I}, \tag{1}$$

where $\mathcal{A}$ is a set of agents and $\mathcal{I}$ represents the values that can be observed. We define $\mathcal{A}' \subseteq \mathcal{A}$ as the minimal subset of agents, dynamically defined by a set of

---

[3] Authors would like to thank anonymous reviewers for raising this issue.

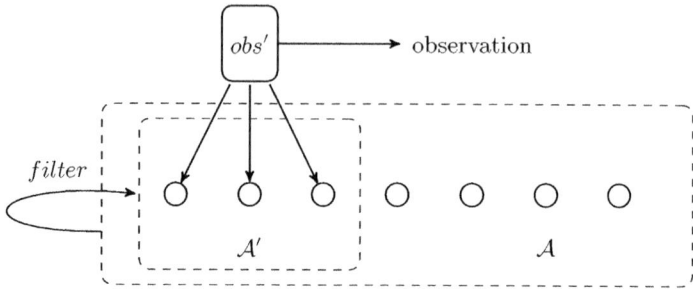

Fig. 3. Filtrated direct observation

constraints (*e.g.*, in the case study, a unique constraint related to the position of the agent), needed to compute *obs* correctly. In other words, $\mathcal{A}'$ is a set of agents such as

$$obs'(\mathcal{A}') = obs(\mathcal{A}) \text{ and}$$
$$\nexists \ \mathcal{A}'' \subset \mathcal{A}' \mid obs'(\mathcal{A}'') = obs(\mathcal{A}), \tag{2}$$

where *obs'* is a "simplified" observation function, *i.e.*, that can be computed faster than *obs* because it is specific to $\mathcal{A}'$:

$$\forall \ \mathcal{A}'' \neq \mathcal{A}' \subseteq \mathcal{A}, \ obs'(\mathcal{A}') = obs(\mathcal{A}'). \tag{3}$$

Thus, in the case study, the observation function $obs(\mathcal{A})$ observes the position of each agent in $\mathcal{A}$ to count only the ones that are situated in $\mathcal{Z}$, while an observation function $obs'(\mathcal{A}')$ would only returns $|\mathcal{A}'|$ because the agents of $\mathcal{A}'$ are by definition situated in $\mathcal{Z}$.

To use *obs'*, it is necessary to consider a filtering function *filter* able to identify the subset $\mathcal{A}'$ (in the case study, this subset only contains the agents situated in $\mathcal{Z}$):

$$filter : 2^{\mathcal{A}} \to 2^{\mathcal{A}} \mid \forall \mathcal{A}', \mathcal{A}'' \subseteq \mathcal{A},$$
$$\text{if } filter(\mathcal{A}') = \mathcal{A}'', \text{ then } \mathcal{A}'' \subseteq \mathcal{A}'. \tag{4}$$

The goal is to define and implement a filtering function, such as the cost of the observation computation is reduced, *i.e.*,

$$\mathcal{C}(obs'(filter(\mathcal{A}))) < \mathcal{C}(obs(\mathcal{A})). \tag{5}$$

In the following section, two different implementations of this idea are presented.

3 Implementation of Filtrated Direct Observation Methods

3.1 Self-observation

The core idea of this method is to implement the filtering function in the simulation agents themselves. Then, using an organizational structure, denoted *group*, allows to identify the set of agents that has to be observed. Thus, a group is defined as *the set of agents that contains the sufficient and necessary information to compute an observation*. In other words, a group defines, for a given observation, the minimal set of agents that is mandatory to compute it. Agents observe themselves to determine if they have to join, leave or stay in a group. A filtering function is defined by a set of rules R, that specifies the conditions under which an agent has to be observed, evaluated at each simulation step (fig. 4).

Thus, in our case study, we consider a group G, that contains the agents situated in $\mathcal{Z}$. The following set of rules, defined here in natural language, is associated to each agent:

- if the agent is in $\mathcal{Z}$ and does not belong to G, then the agent joins G,
- if the agent is not in $\mathcal{Z}$ and belongs to G, then the agent leaves G.

The observation system (obs') only probes the agents of G. Figure 5 presents the CPU time difference between simulations observed with self-observation and brute-force methods as a function of the number of agents in the simulation, N, and the mean rate of observed agents, $E(Z)/N$. The dashed line represents the isoline 0, *i.e.*, the conditions for which there is no difference between the two methods. Thus, the area below this line maps the cases for which self-observation is faster.

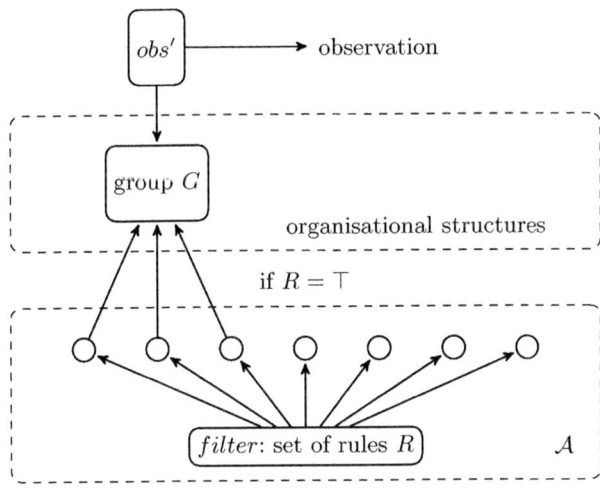

Fig. 4. The self-observation based method

3.2 Statistical Survey

If the equation 2 is rewritten as follows:

$$obs(\mathcal{A}') \simeq obs(\mathcal{A}) \text{ and}$$
$$\nexists \, \mathcal{A}'' \subset \mathcal{A}' \mid obs(\mathcal{A}'') \simeq obs(\mathcal{A}), \tag{6}$$

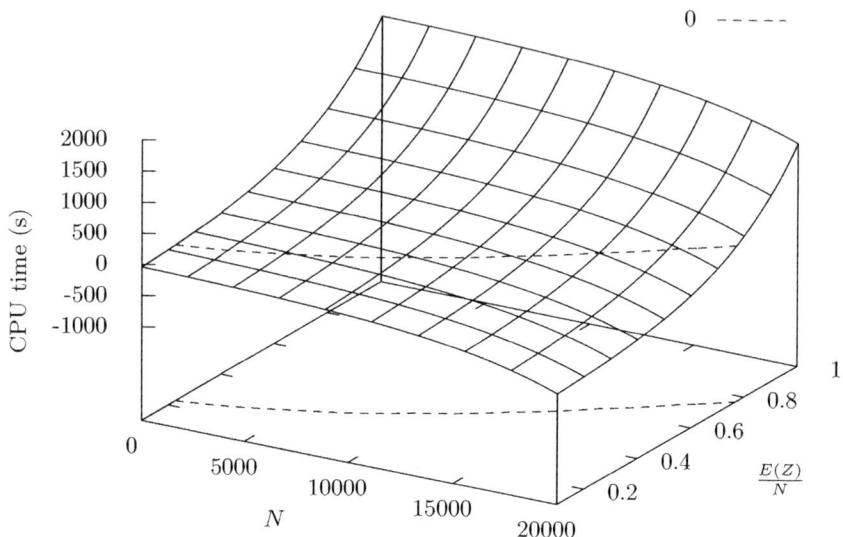

Fig. 5. CPU time difference between simulations observed with self-observation and brute-force methods as a function of the number of agents in the simulation, N, and the mean rate of observed agents, $E(Z)/N$ (response surface estimation)

i.e., if imprecise observations are authorized, it becomes possible to filter the observed population on a statistical basis. As a result, we do not consider a specific observation function anymore as the set of agents returned by the filtering function is not necessary the *set of agents that contains the sufficient and necessary information to compute the observation.*

Statistical survey theory[4] provides a formal ground to determine optimal sampling method and size of observed population sample.

Let once again consider our case study; we denote n the size of the observed population, randomly sampled at each simulation step. An estimator of Z, denoted $\hat{Z}$ is constructed from this sample. Many estimator definitions can be found in the literature. In this case, as the population of simulation agents is homogeneous with respect to $E(Z)$ (all the agents have the same probability to be in $\mathcal{Z}$), n is determined with the Horvitz-Thompson estimator [4] :

$$n^{-1} = \frac{d^2}{4S^2} + \frac{1}{N}, \tag{7}$$

---

[4] Proofs of statistical survey theory results presented in this paper will not be given. Interested readers may refer to [1] for an exhaustive presentation of sampling designs, estimator construction and variability estimation methods.

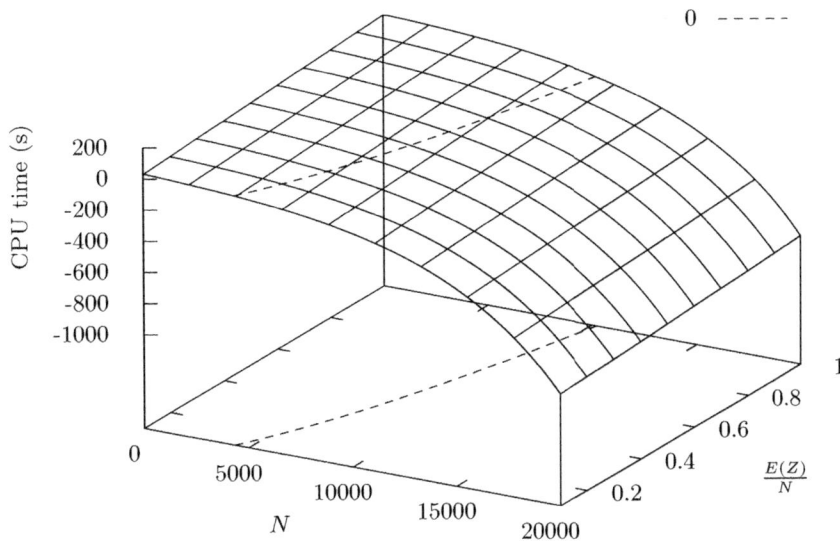

Fig. 6. CPU time difference between simulations observed with statistical survey ($d =$ 0.08) and brute-force methods as a function of the number of agents in the simulation, N, and the mean rate of observed agents, $E(Z)/N$ (response surface estimation)

where d is the maximal absolute error accepted for the observation and

$$S^2 \simeq (1 - \frac{E(Z)}{N}) \cdot \frac{E(Z)}{N}. \tag{8}$$

Impact on the computational cost is shown in figure 6. The semantic is the same than figure 5: the left area maps the cases for which the statistical survey based method is faster than brute-force method.

3.3   Discussion

Figure 7 sums up the previous results qualitatively: conditions for which it is preferable to use one method over another are identified. These results are specific to our case study and its implementation; however, they highlight that the choice of an observation method is not trivial and that the performance of the different available methods should be analyzed on a set of simulations before using the model in a production context.

In a given context, knowing the map of the fastest observation methods allows to dynamically adapt the observation method to use the most efficient one. Impact of dynamic adaptation of the observation method on CPU time is presented in the context of the first example (cf. fig. 2) in figure 8.

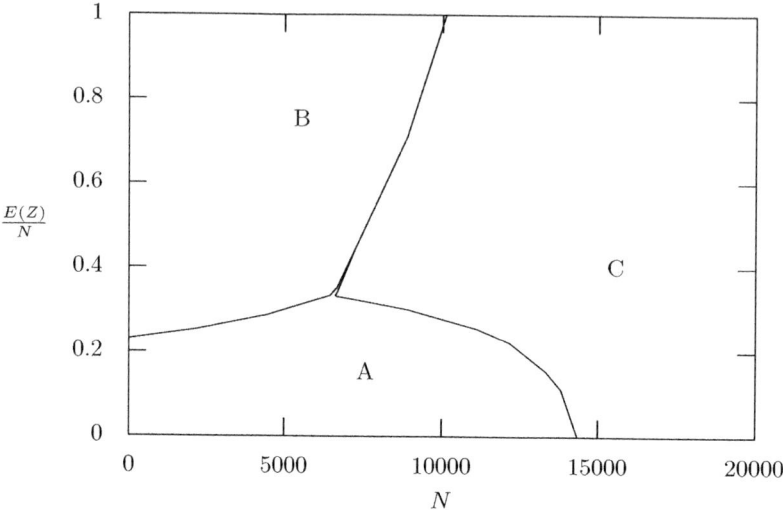

Fig. 7. Map of the fastest observation methods (response surface estimation); A: self-observation, B: brute-force, C: statistical survey ($d = 0.008$)

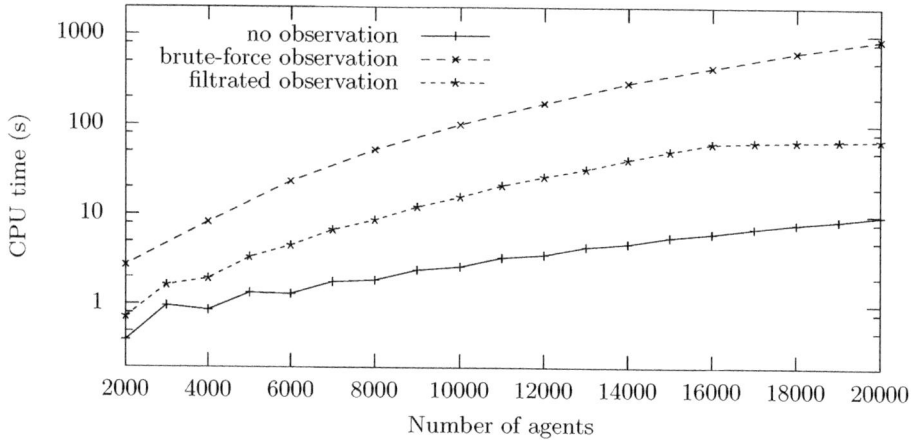

Fig. 8. CPU times (log scale) needed to compute observed and unobserved simulations for $E(Z) = N/5$, filtrated observation method being dynamically adapted to the context

4   Conclusion and Perspectives

Observation methods presented in this paper allow, under specific conditions identified on a simple case study, to reduce significantly the computational cost of MABS composed of numerous agents. However, filtering is not the only option. Considering that imprecise observations are acceptable, while a precision level is guaranteed, the optimal observation frequency could be determined from the observed property variation. Roughly, the more the variation, the more the observation frequency. However, MABS are used to simulate complex systems with nonlinear dynamics. Dynamic adaptation of observation frequency could be an interesting lead to reduce MABS computational cost.

Moreover, in the statistical survey based method (cf. section 3.2), we consider a simple random sampling method, assuming the population is homogeneous. Real world MABS often involve heterogeneous agents for which the distribution of observed individual properties is not uniform. Clever sampling methods, *e.g.*, a stratified random sampling approach, should then be used. In very complex cases, a machine learning system should be implemented to analyze the impact of sampling method properties on the observation quality and computational cost, and determine the optimal ones. Similarly, the organizational model used to implement the self-observation based method is very simple: the only organizational structure that is defined is the "group". Using a more comprehensive one, *e.g.*, AGR [2], would allow to consider very complex and fine observations.

From a methodological point of view, authors experimented that setting up an observation method, generally improves the design of simulation validity metrics. Indeed, it forces simulation designers and users to explicitly define local and global observed properties and their sufficient and necessary conditions of observability, and then the validity constraints over them.

While this paper focuses on reducing the complexity of observation, many published works concentrated on agent interactions by dynamically scaling up and down simulated entities or using more structured interaction artifacts [3,11,8]. Together, these approaches should lead to the conception of highly efficient large-scale MABS simulators.

References

1. Bethlehem, J.: Applied Survey Methods: A Statistical Perspective. Wiley (2009)
2. Ferber, J., Gutknecht, O.: A meta-model for the analysis and design of organizations in multi-agent systems. In: Proceedings of the Third International Conference on Multi-Agent Systems (ICMAS 1998), pp. 128–135 (1998)
3. Gaud, N., Galland, S., Gechter, F., Hilaire, V., Koukam, A.: Holonic multilevel simulation of complex systems: Application to real-time pedestrians simulation in virtual urban environment. Simulation Modelling Practice and Theory 16, 1659–1676 (2008)
4. Horvitz, D.G., Thompson, D.J.: A generalization of sampling without replacement from a finite universe. Journal of the American Statistical Association 47, 663–685 (1952)
5. Kaminka, G., Pynadath, D., Tambe, M.: Monitoring teams by overhearing: A multi-agent planrecognition approach. Journal of Artificial Intelligence 17, 83–135 (2002)
6. Luke, S., Cioffi-Revilla, C., Panait, L., Sullivan, K., Balan, G.: Mason: A multiagent simulation environment. Simulation 81(7), 517–527 (2005)

7. Michel, F., Beurier, G., Ferber, J.: The turtlekit simulation platform: Application to complex systems. In: Proceedings of the First International Conference on Signal-Image Technology and Internet Based Systems, pp. 122–127 (2005)
8. Parunak, H.: Between Agents and Mean Fields. In: Villatoro, D., Sabater-Mir, J., Sichman, J.S. (eds.) MABS 2011. LNCS (LNAI), vol. 7124, pp. 122–135. Springer, Heidelberg (2011)
9. Railsback, S., Lytinen, S., Grimm, V.: Stupidmodel and extensions: A template and teaching tool for agent-based modeling platforms (2005), http://condor.depaul.edu/~slytinen/abm/StupidModelFormulation.pdf
10. Railsback, S., Lytinen, S., Jackson, S.: Agent-based simulation platforms: Review and development recommendations. Simulation 82(9), 609–623 (2006)
11. Razavi, S.N., Gaud, N., Mozayani, N., Koukam, A.: Multi-agent based simulations using fast multipole method: application to large scale simulations of flocking dynamical systems. Artificial Intelligence Review 35(1), 53–72 (2011)
12. Veremme, A., Lefevre, E., Morvan, G., Jolly, D.: Application of the belief function theory to validate multi-agent based simulations. In: First International Workshop on the Theory of Belief Functions (2010)
13. Wilkins, D., Lee, T., Berry, P.: Interactive execution monitoring of agent teams. Journal of Artificial Intelligence Research 18, 217–261 (2003)

Between Agents and Mean Fields

H. Van Dyke Parunak

3520 Green Court, Suite 250
Ann Arbor, MI 48105 USA
van.parunak@jacobs.com

Abstract. Some agent-based models use analogs of insect pheromones for coordination. We situate these techniques in the spectrum of modeling tools. Analysis and simulation show that pheromone models are intermediate between classical agent-based models and mean-field models, inspired by statistical physics. This position is not fixed, but can be adjusted by pheromone parameters (notably, the propagation factor), providing new design options for ABMs.

Keywords: Pheromones, mean-field models, agent-based models.

1 Introduction

Many problems to which agent-based models (ABMs) are applied can also be modeled using mean-field models, typically as differential equations describing the time evolution of system variables. Each type of model has advantages and disadvantages.

One approach to ABM imitates insect pheromones. This paper's central claim is that pheromone-based coordination is intermediate between classical multi-agent systems and mean-field models. Pheromones provide "lumpy-field models": each agent generates a non-uniform field whose mode is related to the agent's location.

We extend a simple model of population dynamics [13] to contrast agents and mean-field models. We analyze this model in both mean-field and conventional agent configurations, to develop intuitions as to the mediating position of pheromone based models. Then we confirm and refine these intuitions using simulations of the system.

Section 2 compares agent-based vs. mean-field models. Section 3 situates pheromone-based coordination in the agent-equation space. An experiment in Section 4 validates and illustrates the claims of Section 3, with special attention to the mapping between computational and physical models of propagation. Section 5 discusses implications of the research, and Section 6 concludes.

2 Agents and Mean Fields

Agent-based modeling is an alternative to equation-based modeling (EBM) [11, 14], in which differential or difference equations capture the evolution of variables. A salient difference [11] is that agent-based modeling directs the modeler's attention to the individual *entities* in the domain, while equation-based models focus on *variables*.

D. Villatoro, J. Sabater-Mir, and J.S. Sichman (Eds.): MABS 2011, LNAI 7124, pp. 113–126, 2012.
© Springer-Verlag Berlin Heidelberg 2012

These variables may be extensive (e.g., the total population or agent density), or intensive (e.g., parameters of individual agents). Intensive variables may reflect individual agents, or (as averages) the system as a whole.

EBM favors extensive variables, or averages over intensive ones, which permit parsimonious closed-form equations. The perspective of such a model is centralized, since such variables require global information. In contrast, the natural tendency in ABM is to define agent behaviors in terms of observables accessible to the individual agent, favoring a local rather than a global viewpoint. The evolution of system-level observables does emerge from an ABM, but the modeler is less likely to use these observables to drive the model's dynamics than in an EBM.

Statistical physics offers an analog to this contrast between local and global information. Systems of many interacting particles are analytically intractable. Physicists consider a single typical particle, and estimate the influence of all the others on it as an average influence. The resulting model is called a "mean-field model" (MFM), because it replaces many individual entities by averages over them.

The canonical example is the Ising model of ferromagnetism [3].An n-dimensional lattice has z sites indexed with i, each with a spin S_i of either $+1$ or -1. These spins are subject to two influences. The first is an external field of strength h. The second is the influence of neighboring spins. The Hamiltonian of the system (roughly, its energy) is

$$E(\{S_i\}) = -h \sum_i S_i - J \sum_{<ij>} S_i S_j \tag{1}$$

where the second sum is over all nearest neighbors and $J > 0$ is the strength of pairwise interactions. The first sum measures the energy due to the interaction of spins with the external field (lowest when aligned, thus negative), and the second sum, the contribution of the nearest neighbor interactions (again lowest when aligned).

In three or more dimensions, this system is analytically intractable. To circumvent this problem, note that the contribution of a single spin to the Hamiltonian is

$$e(S_i) = -hS_i - JS_i \sum S_j \tag{2}$$

summing over all sites adjacent to S_i. The mean field approach replaces the individual S_j's in the summation with their average value $<S_i>$. The contribution of a single site can now be written as a linear function of that site,

$$e_{mf}(S_i) = -hS_i - JS_i \sum <S_j> = -h_{mf}S_i \text{ , where } h_{mf} \equiv h + Jz<S_j> \tag{3}$$

This simplified system is tractable, but neglects the interaction between spins. We have replaced the average of the interactions, $<S_iS_j>$, with the interaction of the averages, $<S_i><S_j>$. This replacement corresponds to an assumption that the spins are statistically independent. In fact, the problem is interesting just because the spins are *not* independent of one another. The consequences of the approximation vary with the dimension of the lattice. In one dimension, it yields qualitatively false results, but as the number of dimensions increases, in spite of the *a priori* unreasonableness of the mean-field assumption, it quantitatively approximates the exact result.

Following this terminology, we describe any model that relies on system-level averages over agent variables as a *mean-field model*. EBMs using extensive and averaged system variables are the most common example of mean-field models, but an agent-based model that uses global knowledge can also do mean-field reasoning. In both cases, the mean-field approach accepts an unrealistic assumption of independence among key variables in exchange for improved tractability.

As in physics, so in multi-agent systems, an MFM has limited accuracy. A given agent parameter may vary widely over the population, and encounters among agents may depend critically on that parameter. Replacing diverse values with a single average may qualitatively change the behavior of the system [13]. Still, MFMs can give concise insight into the behavior of a system that is obscured by discrete models, and researchers increasingly present both models for a system [4, 7].

3   Pheromone-Based Agents

Some social insects coordinate their activities by depositing and sensing chemicals called "pheromones" in a shared environment [15]. Some research in software agents [9] imitates these mechanisms, using a structured environment to implement fundamental information processing tasks. 1) Cells *aggregate* deposits by separate agents, a form of information fusion. 2) Pheromone *propagates* from cells of high concentration to those of low concentration, a form of communication. 3) *Evaporation* discards obsolete information, a primitive form of truth maintenance that runs in constant time (as opposed to NP-complete truth maintenance with non-trivial logics [5]).

Agent-based systems that use these techniques stand in contrast to more traditional AI-based agent models. Both approaches represent entities in the world by software objects that act without being invoked, based on their perception of their environment. They differ in the nature of their interaction with the environment, and in their internal processing. Classical agents maintain explicit representations of other agents in the environment, with whom they often exchange symbolic messages, while pheromone-based agents interact only with the scalar fields that other agents modulate. This focus on numerical as opposed to symbolic representations leads to an emphasis in pheromone-based agents on numerical reasoning (e.g., climbing a weighted combination of observed field strengths), in contrast with the symbolic reasoning characteristic of classical agents.

Digital pheromones were originally used for spatial problems: agents move over a map of the world and the peak of the pheromone field converges to a shortest path [12]. Their quantitative nature makes them seem inappropriate for modeling more complex problems, such as social behavior and human decisions based on symbolic reasoning. In fact, pheromones can be applied to such problems by capturing the logical structure of the problem in the environment over which agents move and in which they deposit and sense pheromones. In traditional behavior modeling, each agent manipulates a logical model inside its head. Pheromone agents handle such problems by externalizing the logical structure and moving over it. An example of this approach is the rTÆMS system for reasoning about plans [2, 8]. In principle, pheromone agents can address any problem that can be represented as a graph.

These mechanisms resemble an MFM. In statistical physics, MFMs simplify computation. Instead of accounting for each particle's interaction with many other particles, we replace the other particles by an average influence, and then compute the behavior of the particle of interest with that average influence. The pheromone field in a pheromone-based agent system is analogous to the average influence in a physical MFM. The field consists of deposits by individual agents. Up to a normalizing constant, this field gives the probability of encountering an agent of the type represented by the field at a given location. When one agent makes decisions based on the field, rather than on explicit representation of other agents, it is reasoning about a weighted average influence of the other agents—weighted because the field is generated by those agents as they move about, and reflects their recent locations.

This weighting is an important refinement over the naïve average in the mean-field approximation to the Ising model in Section 2. Consider one robot coordinating with four others in a 20x20 grid. A naïve mean-field estimate of the probability of encountering another robot in any given cell is 4/400 = 0.01. This probability is isotropic, and so gives no guidance to the robot. At the other extreme, the robot could communicate directly with other robots, remember their most recent locations, and determine with high certainty whether or not a given cell contains another robot.

The pheromone approach is intermediate. Each agent contributes to a field in its vicinity. Other agents in the vicinity also contribute to the field. So the field is an average over multiple agents, but a localized average. This localized average is not just over agents, but also over space and time.

- *Aggregation* collects contributions from multiple agents that are in the same area, averaging over multiple agents. The larger the cells into which the environment is divided, the more agents are included in the average.
- *Propagation* spreads out the deposits, averaging over space. The stronger the propagation, the larger the area of space over which the averaging occurs.
- *Evaporation* determines how long pheromones persist, averaging over time. The stronger the evaporation, the shorter the period over which averaging occurs.

Let's explore the interaction of these dynamics analytically, as they function with chemical pheromones.[1] A single stationary agent at the origin deposits pheromone at a constant rate D. The pheromone field $\varphi(r, t)$ is multiplied by a constant evaporation rate $E \in (0, 1)$ at each time step, thus removing pheromone at a rate $(1 - E)\varphi$, and propagation takes the form of a diffusion process with rate F. We assume a separable solution as a product of spatial and temporal terms of the form $\varphi(\vec{r}, t) = \varphi_s(\vec{r}) \varphi_t(t)$. Empirically, the resulting field reaches equilibrium with a constant strength φ_0 at the origin, providing the boundary condition $\varphi(0, \infty) = \varphi_0$, and this result together with conservation of matter implies $\varphi(\infty, t) = 0$.

The spatial component $\varphi_r (r)$ must satisfy

$$F\nabla^2 \varphi_r - (1 - E)\varphi_r = 0 \qquad (4)$$

That is, the gain in field strength at any location due to propagation of pheromone is balanced by the loss due to evaporation. (4) is the Helmholtz equation

$$\nabla^2 \varphi_r + k^2 \varphi_r = 0 \qquad (5)$$

---

[1] I am grateful to Robert Savit for suggestions in formalizing these dynamics. Unlike [1], and like natural systems, our propagation conserves total pheromone.

with $k = iB$, $B = \sqrt{\frac{1-E}{F}}$. φ_r does not vary with angle, so we use polar coordinates $\vec{r} = (r, \theta)$, for which the solution is a Bessel function. Because k is pure imaginary, we have a modified Bessel function (in this case, of order zero). The boundary condition $\varphi_r(\infty) = 0$ means it is of the second type, $AK_0(Br)$, where A and B are scale factors that do not vary with location and K_n is the modified Bessel function of the second type of order n. In Cartesian coordinates, the corresponding solution would be Ae^{-Br}, and the shape of K_n is similar to e^{-r}, so we call A the amplitude and B the exponent.

This function is undefined at $r = 0$. To achieve the boundary condition $\varphi(0, \infty) = \varphi_0$, we assume that deposits occur in a disk of radius r_0 around the origin, within which density is constant. For comparison with a discrete implementation with cells of unit area, we choose $r_0 = 1/\sqrt{\pi}$, so that the disk corresponds to the cell where the deposit is made. Then we normalize the Bessel function to yield $\varphi(0)$ at the boundary, so

$$\varphi_r(\vec{r}) = \begin{cases} \varphi(0), \; r < r_0 \\ \varphi(0) \frac{K_0(Br)}{K_0(Br_0)}, r \geq r_0 \end{cases} \tag{6}$$

To get φ_0, examine the temporal behavior at $r = 0$. Based on the observed convergence behavior of the system, $\varphi_t(t) = (\alpha - \beta e^{-\gamma t})$, where α is the asymptotic value we seek. So the overall solution will be of the form

$$\varphi(\vec{r}, t) = \begin{cases} \alpha(1 - e^{-\gamma t}), \; r < r_0 \\ \alpha(1 - e^{-\gamma t}) \frac{K_0(Br)}{K_0(Br_0)}, \; r \geq r_0 \end{cases} \tag{7}$$

where the boundary condition $\varphi(r, 0) = 0$ requires $\beta = \alpha$.

As $t \to \infty$, the rate of deposit D into the deposit disk must equal the sum of two flows out of the disc: evaporation (with value $(1 - E)\alpha$), and diffusion (by Fick's law, $FV\varphi$). Integrating the flux around the perimeter of the deposit disk yields

$$\int_0^{2\pi} FV\varphi(r_0) \, r_0 \, d\theta = 2\pi r_0 FV\varphi(r_0)$$
$$= 2\pi r_0 FA\alpha \frac{K_1(Br_0)}{K_0(Br_0)} = 2\pi r_0 \sqrt{F(1-E)}\alpha \frac{K_1(Br_0)}{K_0(Br_0)} \tag{8}$$

So

$$D = (1 - E)\alpha + 2\pi r_0 \sqrt{F(1-E)}\alpha \frac{K_1(Br_0)}{K_0(Br_0)} \tag{9}$$

Solving for the equilibrium concentration α,

$$\alpha = \varphi_0 = \frac{D}{(1-E) + 2\pi r_0 \sqrt{F(1-E)}\alpha \frac{K_1(Br_0)}{K_0(Br_0)}} \tag{10}$$

Thus each agent's contribution to the field is peaked about its location, decaying exponentially with distance. The width of the peak (reflected in the exponent B) depends on the evaporation and propagation rates. Evaporation also localizes the peak temporally. If the agent is moving, it leaves a tear-drop shaped pheromone field, widest and highest near its current location and the tail tracing its recent history.

A pheromone-based agent reasons about other agents, not by tracking their individual locations, but by monitoring their aggregate pheromone field. If it wants to meet another agent, it climbs the field. If it wants to avoid other agents, it moves down the gradient. This process is simpler than monitoring individual agent locations. It is approximate, since each agent's location is represented only by a distribution about its actual location. But the exponential decay of $K_0(r)$ guarantees that that distribution does not become uniform until it evaporates completely. We might say that the agent is using, not a mean-field theory, but a "lumpy-field" theory.

Like the Ising example, the pheromone approach simplifies by discarding information about higher-order interactions. For example, the field representing the other agents does not distinguish them from one another, and so cannot coordinate a strategy that requires the agents to interact in a specified order. This information could be recovered, even in a pheromone model, by maintaining different fields for each agent, increasing processing complexity. Techniques based on parallel exploration of alternative sequences can also address this problem with pheromone-based agents, again requiring additional processing to recover the information lost in the aggregate field.

Now consider the polyagent technique of estimating alternative futures for a Red and Blue avatar and their ghosts. A single Red ghost makes successive moves that require it to decide whether, at each move, its avatar would meet Blue. It estimates the probability of meeting Blue at each move by sampling Blue's pheromone at its location. That pheromone field is generated by multiple Blue ghosts. Red's ghost may simulate successive encounters with Blue at successive time steps, representing a future in which the Red avatar and the Blue avatar repeatedly encounter one another. But the presence of a non-zero Blue pheromone field at successive locations visited by the single Red ghost does *not* guarantee the existence of *any* single future for Blue that visits those locations. Imagine a future in which the first encounter of Red and Blue removes Blue from the system. In this case, it is clearly unrealistic for a Red ghost to simulate a later encounter with Blue. Yet it may encounter Blue pheromone later in its trajectory. The different portions of the field that the Red ghost encounters may have been generated by different Blue ghosts, whose distinct identities have been discarded by the field representation. As in the MFM of the Ising system, the pheromone representation simplifies computation by an independence assumption: it assumes that Blue's future is independent of the encounter with Red, even though the simulation is interesting just because its future is *not* independent of Red.

In spite of this simplification, polyagents can forecast the trajectory of complex systems better than other computational techniques with which they have been compared, and better than human experts [6]. The reason appears to be that the ghosts can explore far more alternatives than humans can keep in mind at one time, and take account of the interactions among agents better than other computational techniques.

4   An Experiment

We illustrate the lumpy-field nature of pheromone-based systems with a simulation experiment [13] that contrasts the behavior of a system of discrete agents with a set of differential equations that capture the mean-field behavior. A pheromone version shows behavior intermediate between the other two models.

4.1   Description of Experiment

A toroidal arena hosts two species of agents. Species I is immortal, uniformly distributed with average density n_I, and diffuses with diffusion coefficient D_I. Species M is mortal, with initial uniform density n_M. Mortal agents die at a constant rate μ, divide with rate λ when they encounter an immortal, and diffuse with coefficient D_M.

Continuity and symmetry predict that immortals will remain homogeneously distributed, $n_I(x) = n_I$. The time evolution of n_M is represented by

$$\frac{\partial n_M}{\partial t} = D_M \nabla^2 n_M + (\lambda n_I - \mu)n_M \tag{11}$$

For initially uniform spatial distributions of both species, the solution is

$$n_M(t) = n_M(0)e^{t(\lambda n_I - \mu)} \tag{12}$$

If $\lambda n_I < \mu$, mortals will become extinct.

An agent-based simulation (NetLogo, Table 1) shows different behavior.

Table 1. General Parameters for NetLogo Simulations

Parameter	Value
Arena size	81 x 81 cells
Immortal population	50
Immortal diffusion	0.14
Mortal population	150
Mortal diffusion	0.11

Fig. 1 plots the population of mortals over time for $\mu - \lambda n_I = 0.3$, a regime in which Equation (12) predicts extinction. Instead, the mortal population explodes.

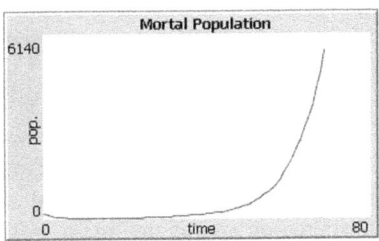

Fig. 1. Mortal Population, ABM

The difference between models is due to a mean-field assumption in the EBM. Overall, immortal agents are homogeneously distributed, but as sampled by mortal agents, they are not. Mortals are born only when a mortal encounters an immortal, and come into existence close to an immortal. The density of immortals *near mortals* is far greater than n_I. Fig. 2 shows a screen shot at the end of Fig 1. Three immortals form breeding clusters that generate mortals faster than they can die.

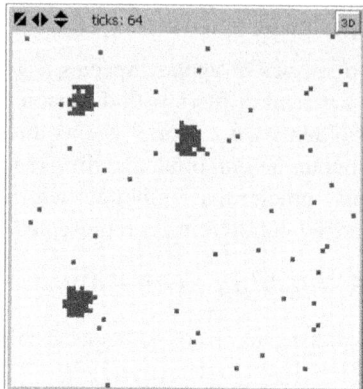

Fig. 2. Breeding clusters. The dark clumped agents are mortals; the scattered agents are immortals.

Not every run with $\lambda n_I < \mu$ explodes. The outcome depends on location in parameter space, and stochasticity. Several system parameters are implemented as stochastic choices by each agent, including birth rate, death rate, and diffusion. For example, a moral who meets an immortal samples a uniform distribution on [0, 1] and gives birth only if the result is less than or equal to λ. In different runs, these stochastic decisions can yield different outcomes. In addition, different parameters affect mortal survival, by determining the viability of a breeding cluster.

- With too few agents, a mortal may die before meeting an immortal and breeding.
- If the birth rate is too low, losses due to diffusion and death outpace births.
- If the mortal diffusion rate is too high, new mortals drift away from the immortal parent so fast that the breeding cluster disintegrates.

We observe the effects of these parameters by analyzing repeated runs. Empirically, if $n_M > 1000$, the system explodes. So we run until either $n_M = 0$ or $n_M > 1000$. We repeat each configuration 25 times with different random seeds, and record the percentage of trials in which n_M goes to zero.

Fig. 3 shows the percentage of runs ("pct") in which mortals survive as a function of birth and death rates. $\lambda n_I - \mu$ ranges from 0 to -0.5, except when the death rate is zero, in which case the difference is in [0.004, 0.008]. Toward the front of the figure (low birth rate and high death rate), virtually all runs end in extinction. This region is nearly flat until one reaches a region around the line $\mu = 0.6\lambda - 0.2$. Then the probability rises rapidly to the corner with high birth rates and low death rates.

Survival or extinction does depend on a balance between birth and death rates (Fig. 3), but birth rate has more influence than in the MFM. $\partial\mu/\partial\lambda$ along the edge of the region where the agent-based model differs from the MFM is 0.6, while the corresponding value in the equation, n_I, is $50/81^2 \cong 0.0076$. The simulation behaves as though the density of mortals were nearly 100 times greater than n_M. Factors like mortal population and rate of diffusion modulate this effect (Fig. 4). Low initial mortal population and high diffusion lead to extinction; the opposite corner leads to survival.

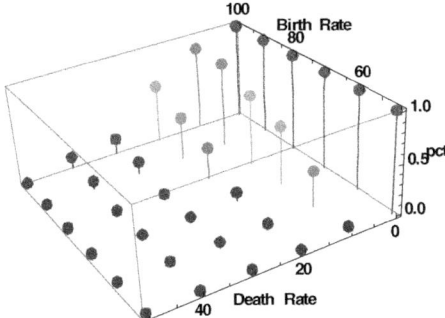

Fig. 3. Survival probability ("pct"=percent surviving) as function of birth and death rates

4.2   Adaptation for Pheromone-Based Agents

In both models, the probability $p(birth)$ that a mortal gives birth is $p(parent)*\lambda$. λ is just the probability of a birth conditioned on the presence of an immortal parent. $p(parent)$ is the probability that a parent is present. The models differ in how they estimate $p(parent)$. For the MFM, $p(parent) = n_I$. In the discrete agent model,

$$p(parent) = \begin{cases} 1 \ if \ immortal \ is \ in \ cell \\ 0 \ otherwise \end{cases} \tag{13}$$

(If a cell contains multiple immortals, the computation is repeated for each.)

Pheromones offer an intermediate "lumpy-field" approach with simpler computation than the discrete model and more accuracy than the mean field approach.

Each immortal deposits one unit of pheromone per step at its location. The total deposit per step is n_I. Each mortal samples the field φ at its location, estimates $p(parent)$, and computes $p(birth)$. If $\varphi > 1$, the mortal behaves as though it encountered $\lfloor \varphi \rfloor$ immortals, plus one more with probability $\varphi - \lfloor \varphi \rfloor$. A single deposit by stationary immortals and no evaporation or propagation recovers the discrete model.

Constant deposit and exponential evaporation lead to an asymptotic fixed point. By setting the deposit rate to 1 per immortal and evaporation to 0.5, the total pheromone is constant, and equal to the immortal population. With stationary immortals and no propagation, this configuration also recovers the discrete model.

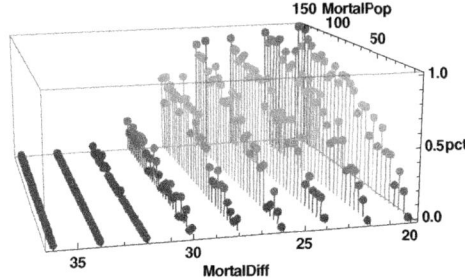

Fig. 4. Observed probability of survival as function of mortal diffusion rate and initial population

When immortals move, or when we allow propagation, the field extends beyond the cell containing the immortal. This spreading can allow an invalid birth: a mortal may think it is in the presence of an immortal when it is not. As in the Ising model, increased error is the cost of simpler computation.

We use NetLogo's *diffuse* function for propagation. *diffuse* takes an argument ρ in [0,1], subtracts $\rho * \varphi$ from each cell, and distributes $\rho * \varphi$ evenly among the cell's eight neighbors, conserving the total field. The function is applied to all cells at once.

Propagation modeled on chemical diffusion in an insect system (4) is a function of the second derivative of φ, not its absolute strength. NetLogo's *diffuse* operator (like most implementations of digital pheromones) depends only on the local strength of the field and relies on exchanges from neighboring cells to incorporate information analogous to the local derivative. So we need to qualify our claim that the NetLogo implementation represents propagation. The two processes share some features: the form of (6) is a good fit to the fixed point of the observed distribution. But quantitatively, the correspondence is weaker.

Under the dubious mapping $F = \rho$, *diffuse* yields an exponent related to the exponent $B = \sqrt{\frac{1-E}{F}}$, but an amplitude less clearly related to (10). Fig. 5a plots observed vs. theoretical amplitude. The theory is off by more than an order of magnitude. Fig. 5b plots the ratio of observed exponent *obs* to theoretical exponent *the*. This relationship is closer, a good fit to $\frac{obs}{the} = 2.27(e^{0.35\,obs} - 1)$, but hardly constant, much less 1. Nevertheless, we press ahead.

As ρ increases, a pheromone model should behave less like a discrete model and more like an MFM. Because of the lumpiness of the field, the resulting error will never be as bad as in the MFM, as Fig. 6 shows. As ρ increases, the probability of survival approaches zero everywhere except when $\mu = 0$, as in the MFM.

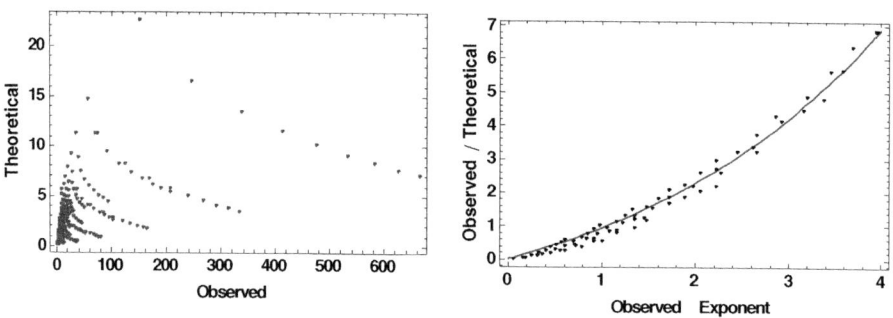

Fig. 5. a (left): Relation between observed and theoretical amplitude. b (right): Relation between observed and theoretical exponent.

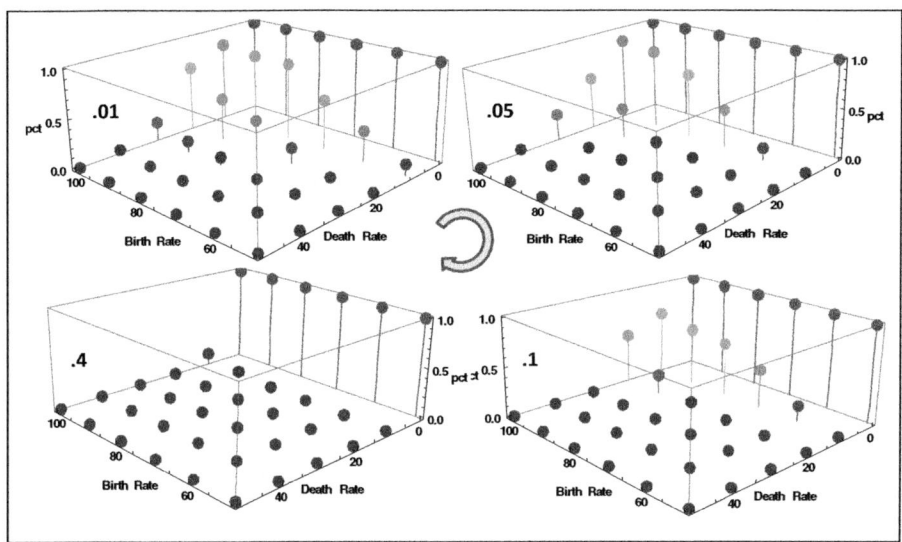

Fig. 6. Survival, propagation = (from top left, clockwise) 0.01, 0.05, 0.1, 0.4

We can quantify this difference. Each scenario (mean-field and pheromone with various diffusion rates) yields survival rates as a function of λ and μ that differ from the discrete agent system. We weight these differences by the differences observed in the MFM, and normalize by the sum of these weights. On this scale, the MFM scores 1, and the discrete agent system scores 0. Fig. 7 shows this score as a function of propagation. As anticipated, the error grows with propagation rate, and asymptotes before it reaches the mean-field level.

In Fig. 7, error *increases* when diffusion is 0, compared with 0.01. We expect to recover the discrete model in this case. The difference is that propagation of 0 corresponds to the discrete model only if the agent depositing the pheromone is stationary. Our immortal agents move occasionally, and may leave behind a deposit that can mislead mortals. Propagation, as well as evaporation, reduces this obsolete information. To confirm this effect, we run the system with stationary immortals, and obtain the error scores in Table 2. Now propagation 0 does indeed yield error less than 0.01,

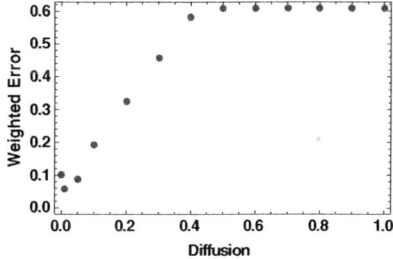

Fig. 7. Dependence of weighted error on diffusion

and almost achieves the 0 score of discrete agents. (The residual error is due to the difference between stochastic decisions in the pheromone agent and deterministic ones in the discrete agents.)

Table 2. Error for Stationary Agents

Configuration	Weighted Error
Discrete agents	0 (by definition)
Propagation 0	0.079
Propagation 0.01	0.160

5   Discussion

Both analysis and simulation show that pheromone-based agents are intermediate between MFMs and conventional agents. Such mediating techniques provide a richer array of techniques to balance computational complexity and model fidelity. At the same time, the richer the toolbox, the more skills are required to use it. Though preliminary, our results suggest some guidelines concerning the use of pheromone systems.

Pheromones can reduce fidelity. When agents base decisions on fields rather than on direct observation, they make independence assertions that may violate the structure of the problem. Whether these violations are empirically meaningful is problem-dependent. In practice, pheromones often yield very useful results. We speculate that just as the mean-field analysis of the Ising model becomes more accurate as dimensionality increases, the high dimensionality of many domains to which pheromones are often applied makes the violations less significant.

Two conditions recommend pheromone methods: problem complexity and the need for statistical estimates.

A conventional ABM may require much knowledge engineering, computational effort, or both, making pheromones attractive. Still, the approach is a heuristic, and validation against domain-specific experiments (e.g., [6]) is essential.

Statistically, many domains require estimating alternative outcomes. The space of outcomes is often so large that even thousands of replications of a conventional agent model may not give a meaningful sample [10]. This requirement is a clear indicator for the polyagent technique of virtual or "ghost" agents that interact indirectly through fields summarizing the distribution over multiple futures of each agent.

One benefit of pheromones over an EBM is the ability to tune fidelity using propagation, which governs the degree of spatial averaging over agents. (We can also tune using the evaporation rate, adjusting the degree of temporal averaging.) Lower propagation improves fidelity (Fig. 7). Models more complex than ours may show a trade-off between fidelity and other characteristics (e.g., stability or convergence).

Finally, comparison of a representative computational analog of propagation (NetLogo's *diffuse* operator) with the physical diffusion that propagates insect pheromones shows qualitative similarity between the mechanisms, and suggestive though non-trivial quantitative relations with the exponent of the spatial decay and the asymptotic amplitude of the temporal stabilization that merit further study.

6   Conclusion

MFMs simplify the computational burden of tracking detailed multi-agent interactions by replacing individual interactions with statistical summaries of the population from the perspective of a single agent. This simplification imposes unwarranted independence assumptions. In spite of these assumptions, the results are useful often enough that these models continue to be widely used.

Conventional ABMs compute each interaction, yielding higher accuracy than an MFM, but the computational burden precludes thorough sampling.

Pheromone-based constructs such as the polyagent reduce the computational cost of modeling the space of interactions. There is no free lunch. This simplification (as in the corresponding physics theories) can usually be described as an independence assumption. Because the agent framework retains the discrete structure of the problem, the resulting error is often much less than in a complete mean-field treatment, and can be tuned by adjusting the degree of propagation of the pheromones.

Table 3 offers a summary comparison of the three approaches.

Table 3. Comparison of Types of Models

Model Type	Representation of Non-Self Agents	Interactions	Computational Cost	Error
Classical MAS	Explicit	Direct	High	Low
Pheromones	Lumpy field	Indirect, non-uniform	Medium	Medium
Mean-field	Uniform field	Uniform	Low	High

Recognizing the mediating position of pheromone models between conventional agents and equation-based MFMs allows modelers to make more appropriate use of this promising technology.

References

1. Brueckner, S.: Return from the Ant: Synthetic Ecosystems for Manufacturing Control. Thesis at Humboldt University Berlin, Department of Computer Science (2000)
2. Brueckner, S., Belding, T., Bisson, R., Downs, E., Parunak, H.V.D.: Swarming Polyagents Executing Hierarchical Task Networks. In: Proceedings of Third IEEE International Conference on Self-Adaptive and Self-Organizing Systems (SASO 2009), pp. 51–60. IEEE (2009)
3. Evans, M.: MP4/P4 Statistical Physics. University of Edinburgh, Edinburgh, UK (2009), http://www2.ph.ed.ac.uk/~martin/sp/

4. Glinton, R., Scerri, P., Sycara, K.: Exploiting Scale Invariant Dynamics for Efficient Information Propagation in Large Teams. In: Hoek, W.V.D., Kaminka, G.A. (eds.) The Ninth International Conference on Autonomous Agents and Multi-Agent Systems (AAMAS 2010), pp. 21–28. IFAAMAS, Toronto (2010)
5. Levesque, H.J., Brachman, R.J.: Expressiveness and Tractability in Knowledge Representation and Reasoning. Computational Intelligence 3(2), 78–93 (1987)
6. Parunak, H.V.D.: Real-Time Agent Characterization and Prediction. In: Proceedings of International Joint Conference on Autonomous Agents and Multi-Agent Systems (AAMAS 2007), Industrial Track, pp. 1421–1428. ACM (2007)
7. Parunak, H.V.D.: A Mathematical Analysis of Collective Cognitive Convergence. In: Proceedings of the Eighth International Conference on Autonomous Agents and Multi-Agent Systems (AAMAS 2009), pp. 473–480 (2009)
8. Parunak, H.V.D., Bisson, R., Brueckner, S.A.: Agent Interaction, Multiple Perspectives, and Swarming Simulation. In: Proceedings of the International Joint Conference on Autonomous Agents and Multi-Agent Systems (AAMAS 2010), pp. 549–556. IFAAMAS (2010)
9. Parunak, H.V.D., Brueckner, S.: Ant-Like Missionaries and Cannibals: Synthetic Pheromones for Distributed Motion Control. In: Proceedings of Fourth International Conference on Autonomous Agents (Agents 2000), pp. 467–474 (2000)
10. Van Dyke Parunak, H., Brueckner, S.A.: Concurrent Modeling of Alternative Worlds with Polyagents. In: Antunes, L., Takadama, K. (eds.) MABS 2006. LNCS (LNAI), vol. 4442, pp. 128–141. Springer, Heidelberg (2007)
11. Van Dyke Parunak, H., Savit, R., Riolo, R.L.: Agent-Based Modeling vs. Equation-Based Modeling: A Case Study and Users' Guide. In: Sichman, J.S., Conte, R., Gilbert, N. (eds.) MABS 1998. LNCS (LNAI), vol. 1534, pp. 10–25. Springer, Heidelberg (1998)
12. Sauter, J.A., Matthews, R., Parunak, H.V.D., Brueckner, S.A.: Performance of Digital Pheromones for Swarming Vehicle Control. In: Proceedings of Fourth International Joint Conference on Autonomous Agents and Multi-Agent Systems, pp. 903–910. ACM (2005)
13. Shnerb, N.M., Louzoun, Y., Bettelheim, E., Solomon, S.: The importance of being discrete: Life always wins on the surface. Proc. Natl. Acad. Sci. USA 97(19), 10322–10324 (2000)
14. Sterman, J.: Business Dynamics. McGraw-Hill, New York (2000)
15. Wilson, E.O., Bossert, W.H.: Chemical communication among animals. Recent Progress in Hormone Research 19, 673–716 (1963)

Author Index

Batch number: 09478804

Printed by Printforce, the Netherlands